D0846505

Securing the vote
Protecting American Democracy

Committee on the Future of Voting:
Accessible, Reliable, Verifiable Technology

Committee on Science, Technology, and Law

Policy and Global Affairs

Computer Science and Telecommunications Board

Division on Engineering and Physical Sciences

A Consensus Study Report of

The National Academies of
SCIENCES · ENGINEERING · MEDICINE

THE NATIONAL ACADEMIES PRESS
Washington, DC
www.nap.edu

THE NATIONAL ACADEMIES PRESS   500 Fifth Street, NW   Washington, DC 20001

This activity was supported with grants to the National Academy of Sciences from the Carnegie Corporation of New York (#G-16-53637) and the William and Flora Hewlett Foundation (#G-2016-5031) and with funds from National Academy of Sciences' W. K. Kellogg Foundation Fund and the National Academies of Sciences, Engineering, and Medicine's Presidents' Circle Fund. Any opinions, findings, conclusions, or recommendations expressed in this publication do not necessarily reflect the views of any organization or agency that provided support for the project.

International Standard Book Number-13: 978-0-309-47647-8
International Standard Book Number-10: 0-309-47647-X
Library of Congress Control Number: 2018952779
Digital Object Identifier: https://doi.org/10.17226/25120

Additional copies of this publication are available for sale from the National Academies Press, 500 Fifth Street, NW, Keck 360, Washington, DC 20001; (800) 624-6242 or (202) 334-3313; http://www.nap.edu.

Printed in the United States of America

Suggested citation: National Academies of Sciences, Engineering, and Medicine. 2018. *Securing the Vote: Protecting American Democracy*. Washington, DC: The National Academies Press. doi: https://doi.org/10.17226/25120.

The National Academies of
SCIENCES · ENGINEERING · MEDICINE

The **National Academy of Sciences** was established in 1863 by an Act of Congress, signed by President Lincoln, as a private, nongovernmental institution to advise the nation on issues related to science and technology. Members are elected by their peers for outstanding contributions to research. Dr. Marcia McNutt is president.

The **National Academy of Engineering** was established in 1964 under the charter of the National Academy of Sciences to bring the practices of engineering to advising the nation. Members are elected by their peers for extraordinary contributions to engineering. Dr. C. D. Mote, Jr., is president.

The **National Academy of Medicine** (formerly the Institute of Medicine) was established in 1970 under the charter of the National Academy of Sciences to advise the nation on medical and health issues. Members are elected by their peers for distinguished contributions to medicine and health. Dr. Victor J. Dzau is president.

The three Academies work together as the **National Academies of Sciences, Engineering, and Medicine** to provide independent, objective analysis and advice to the nation and conduct other activities to solve complex problems and inform public policy decisions. The National Academies also encourage education and research, recognize outstanding contributions to knowledge, and increase public understanding in matters of science, engineering, and medicine.

Learn more about the National Academies of Sciences, Engineering, and Medicine at **www.nationalacademies.org**.

The National Academies of
SCIENCES · ENGINEERING · MEDICINE

Consensus Study Reports published by the National Academies of Sciences, Engineering, and Medicine document the evidence-based consensus on the study's statement of task by an authoring committee of experts. Reports typically include findings, conclusions, and recommendations based on information gathered by the committee and the committee's deliberations. Each report has been subjected to a rigorous and independent peer-review process and it represents the position of the National Academies on the statement of task.

Proceedings published by the National Academies of Sciences, Engineering, and Medicine chronicle the presentations and discussions at a workshop, symposium, or other event convened by the National Academies. The statements and opinions contained in proceedings are those of the participants and are not endorsed by other participants, the planning committee, or the National Academies.

For information about other products and activities of the National Academies, please visit www.nationalacademies.org/about/whatwedo.

Staff

ANNE-MARIE MAZZA, Study Director and Senior Director, Committee on Science, Technology, and Law
JON EISENBERG, Senior Director, Computer Science and Telecommunications Board
STEVEN KENDALL, Program Officer, Committee on Science, Technology, and Law
KAROLINA KONARZEWSKA, Program Coordinator, Committee on Science, Technology, and Law
WILLIAM J. SKANE, Consultant Writer
CLARA SAVAGE, Financial Officer, Committee on Science, Technology, and Law

COMMITTEE ON SCIENCE, TECHNOLOGY, AND LAW

Staff

JON EISENBERG, Senior Director
LYNETTE I. MILLETT, Associate Director and Director, Forum on
    Cyber Resilience
EMILY GRUMBLING, Program Officer
KATIRIA ORTIZ, Associate Program Officer
JANKI PATEL, Senior Program Assistant
SHENAE BRADLEY, Administrative Assistant
RENEE HAWKINS, Financial and Administrative Manager

Preface

When we were asked in fall 2016 to serve as co-chairs of the committee that would ultimately author the current report, it seemed that our attention would be focused on identifying technological solutions that could redress problems such as long lines at polling places and outdated election systems. We imagined that we would offer an evaluation of the innovations being adopted by forward-looking election administrators across the nation. We suspected that we would find that voting systems are moving away from in-person physical balloting toward systems that embrace technologies that enable remote (Internet) voting.

However, by the time the committee met for the first time in April 2017, it was clear that the most significant threat to the American elections system was coming, not from faulty or outdated technologies, but from efforts to undermine the credibility of election results. Unsubstantiated claims about election outcomes fanned by social and other media threaten civic stability. Perhaps even more troubling is evidence that foreign actors are targeting our election infrastructure in an attempt to undermine confidence in our democratic institutions. On a regular, almost daily basis, we learned more about the nature of and motives behind this new and dangerous development. Even as we received testimony from election administrators and experts from government, industry, and academia regarding the many issues faced in the conduct of elections, we were constantly reminded in news stories, by congressional hearings, and through reports from the intelligence community of the extraordinary threat from foreign actors using cyber weapons and social media to manipulate the electorate and to target our elections and cast doubt on the integrity of the elections process.

The current report makes numerous recommendations designed to harden our election infrastructure and safeguard its integrity and credibility.

We live in a nation that is unique in the tremendous importance it places on free speech. This remarkable privilege was enshrined in the First Amendment by the framers of the Constitution. Not only does the Constitution forbid official censorship, but it invests our government with the extraordinary responsibility of ensuring that all Americans can be heard. In this context, the ability of the citizenry to participate in elections and have their votes accurately cast and counted is paramount.

Over the course of this study, we were inspired by dedicated and enlightened election officials from across the nation and all levels of government. Such individuals are working tirelessly to improve accessibility, harness new technologies, and ensure the integrity of the results of elections. Unfortunately, these same officials often lack appropriate staff and resources and are routinely hampered in their work by a patchwork of laws and regulations that make it difficult to upgrade and modernize their election systems.

We also heard from researchers working to design better ballots, develop better and more secure voting systems, and identify new ways to quickly and reliably certify that the results of elections are reflective of the will of the voters. All too often, their efforts are underfunded, important research questions remain unaddressed, and there are challenges to translating research into practice.

The 2016 Presidential election was a watershed moment in the history of elections. The election exposed new technical and operational challenges that require the immediate attention of state and local governments, the federal government, researchers, and the American public. The election showed us that citizens must become more discerning consumers of information and that state and local governments must work collaboratively and together with the federal government to secure our election systems. Further, our leaders must speak candidly and apolitically about threats to our election systems. Transparent communication about threats to the integrity of our elections is vital. Openness is the most effective antidote to cynicism and distrust. In the interconnected world we increasingly live in, we want and need to hear what those beyond our borders think, but we must be cognizant of deliberate and deceitful efforts to spread disinformation and propaganda. The American people must have confidence that their leaders place the larger interests of democracy above all else. The future of voting is one in which a clear tension must be managed: we must prevent bad actors from corrupting our electoral process while delivering the means to provide suffrage to an electorate that is growing in size and complexity.

We are deeply indebted to the members of the committee for their dedication to our task and for the countless hours they spent exchanging ideas and reviewing testimony and background materials. Each member contributed thoughtfully and collegially to the committee's many discussions.

We are immensely grateful to the staff who worked tirelessly on behalf of the committee: Anne-Marie Mazza; Jon Eisenberg; Steven Kendall; Karolina Konarzewska; and consultant writer Bill Skane.

It has been our great pleasure and honor to lead this important study. We believe that the findings and recommendations laid out in this report provide the United States with a blueprint for an elections system that is accessible, reliable, verifiable, and secure.

Lee C. Bollinger and Michael A. McRobbie
Committee Co-chairs

Acknowledgments

ACKNOWLEDGMENT OF PRESENTERS

The committee gratefully acknowledges the thoughtful contributions of the following individuals who made presentations before the committee: Robert F. Bauer, Perkins Coie LLP; Brenda Bayes, State of Oregon; David Becker, Center for Election Innovation & Research; David Beirne, Federal Voting Assistance Program; Kenneth Bennett, Los Angeles County, CA; Matthew Blaze, University of Pennsylvania; Mary Brady, National Institute of Standards and Technology; Jonathan Brill, Scytl; Matthew Caulfied, University of Pennsylvania; Doug Chapin, University of Minnesota; Edgardo Cortes, State of Virginia Elections Board; McDermot Coutts, Unisyn Voting Solutions; David Fidler, Indiana University; Monica Flores, Los Angeles County, CA; Joe P. Gloria, Clark County, NV; Diane Cordry Golden, Association of Assistive Technology Act Programs; J. Alex Halderman, University of Michigan; Geoffrey Hale, U.S. Department of Homeland Security; Kathleen Hale, Auburn University; Hillary Hall, Boulder County, CO; Thad Hall, Fors Marsh Group; Shane Hamlin, Electronic Registration Information Center (ERIC); Jackie Harris, Democracy Live; General Michael Hayden, U.S. Air Force, National Security Agency, and Central Intelligence Agency (retired); Susan Hennessey, Brookings Institution; Douglas A. Kellner, State of New York; Merle King, Kennesaw State University; Joe Kiniry, Free & Fair; Robert Kolasky, U.S. Department of Homeland Security; Connie Lawson, State of Indiana and National Association of Secretaries of State; Matthew Masterson, U.S. Election Assistance Commission; Tim Mattice, The Election Center; Neal McBurnett,

Free & Fair; Amber McReynolds, City and County of Denver, CO; Jennifer Morrell, Arapahoe County, CO; Jessica Myers, U.S. Election Assistance Commission; Brian Newby, U.S. Election Assistance Commission; Lawrence Norden, Brennan Center for Justice at New York University; Alex Padilla, National Association of Secretaries of State; Eddie Perez, Hart InterCivic; Whitney Quesenbery, Center for Civic Design; Peggy Reeves, State of Connecticut; Leslie Reynolds, National Association of Secretaries of State; Robert Rock, State of Rhode Island; Hilary Rudy, State of Colorado; John Schmitt, Five Cedars Group; Lisa Schur, Rutgers University; Alexander Schwarzmann, University of Connecticut; Will Senning, State of Vermont; James Simons, Everyone Counts; David Stafford, Escambia County (FL) Elections Office; Robert M. Stein, Rice University; and Anthony Stevens, State of New Hampshire.

ACKNOWLEDGMENT OF REVIEWERS

This Consensus Study Report was reviewed in draft form by individuals chosen for their diverse perspectives and technical expertise. The purpose of this independent review is to provide candid and critical comments that will assist the National Academies of Sciences, Engineering, and Medicine in making each published report as sound as possible and to ensure that it meets the institutional standards for quality, objectivity, evidence, and responsiveness to the study charge. The review comments and draft manuscript remain confidential to protect the integrity of the deliberative process.

We thank the following individuals for their review of this report: Robert Bauer, Perkins Coie LLP; Matthew Blaze, University of Pennsylvania; Douglas Chapin, University of Minnesota; Judd Choate, Colorado Department of State; David Dill, Stanford University; J. Alex Halderman, University of Michigan; Michael Hass, Wisconsin Election Commission; Douglas Kellner, New York State Board of Elections; Philip Kortum, Rice University; Jane Lute, United Nations; Whitney Quesenbery, Center for Civic Design; Barbara Simons, IBM Corporation; David Stafford, Escambia County (FL) Elections Office; and Philip Stark, University of California, Berkeley.

Although the reviewers listed above provided many constructive comments and suggestions, they were not asked to endorse the conclusions or recommendations of this report nor did they see the final draft before its release. The review of this report was overseen by Anita K. Jones, University of Virginia and David C. Vladeck, Georgetown University Law Center. They were responsible for making certain that an independent examination of this report was carried out in accordance with the standards of the National Academies and that all review comments were carefully considered. Responsibility for the final content rests entirely with the authoring committee and the National Academies.

Contents

Boxes, Figures, and Tables

BOXES

FIGURES

TABLES

Summary

During the 2016 presidential election, America's election infrastructure was targeted by a foreign government.[1] According to assessments by members of the U.S. Intelligence Community,[2] actors sponsored by the Russian government "obtained and maintained access to elements of multiple US state or local electoral boards."[3] While the full

---

[1] For the purposes of this report, *election infrastructure* is defined as the physical and organizational structures and facilities and personnel needed for the operation of elections.

[2] The U.S. Intelligence Community consists of 16 agencies working under the coordination of the Office of the Director of National Intelligence. The 16 agencies are the: Central Intelligence Agency; Defense Intelligence Agency; Federal Bureau of Investigation; National Geospatial-Intelligence Agency; National Reconnaissance Office; National Security Agency/Central Security Service; U.S. Department of Energy; U.S. Department of Homeland Security (DHS); U.S. Department of State; U.S. Department of the Treasury; Drug Enforcement Administration; U.S. Air Force; U.S. Army; U.S. Coast Guard; U.S. Marine Corps; and U.S. Navy.

[3] The U.S. Department of Homeland Security (DHS) assessed "**that the types of systems Russian actors targeted or compromised were not involved in vote tallying.**" See Office of the Director of National Intelligence, "Assessing Russian Activities and Intentions in Recent US Elections, Intelligence Community Assessment," January 6, 2017, p. iii, available at: https://www.dni.gov/files/documents/ICA_2017_01.pdf. Bolded text is original to the document.

By September 2017, voter registration systems or public election sites in 21 states had been identified by DHS as having been targeted by Russian hackers. See, e.g., National Association of Secretaries of State, "NASS Statement on US Department of Homeland Security (DHS) Outreach to 21 States Regarding Potential Targeting," September 25, 2017, available at: https://www.nass.org/node/284 and Horwitz, Sari, Ellen Nakashima, and Matea Gold, "DHS Tells States About Russian Hacking During 2016 Election," *Washington Post*, September 22, 2017.

Voter registration systems and public election websites (e.g., state "my voter" pages) are *election systems*. For the purposes of this report, election system is defined as a technology-based

extent and impact of these activities is not known and our understanding of these events is evolving, there is little doubt that these efforts represented an assault on the American system of representative democracy.

The vulnerability of election infrastructure to cyberattacks became a growing concern during the campaign leading up to the 2016 presidential election, and in fall 2016, the federal government took the unusual step of issuing a joint statement from the U.S. Department of Homeland Security (DHS) and the Office of the Director of National Intelligence (ODNI) urging state and local governments to be "vigilant and seek cybersecurity assistance from DHS."[4] In late December 2016, as the extent of Russian activities became apparent, President Barack Obama invoked sanctions against Russia for its efforts to disrupt the presidential election.[5] In early 2017, the nation's election systems were given critical infrastructure status.[6]

---

system that is used to collect, process, and store data related to elections and election administration. In addition to voter registration systems and public election websites, election systems include voting systems (the means through which voters cast their ballots), vote tabulation systems, election night reporting systems, and auditing systems.

Whether there were attacks on voting systems or vote tabulation systems is unknown. The committee authoring this report is not aware of an ongoing investigation into this possibility. In 2016, gaps in intelligence gathering, information sharing, and reporting led to problems that were underappreciated at the time of the intrusions leaving considerable uncertainty about what happened, even today. See, e.g., U.S. Senate Select Committee on Intelligence, "Russian Targeting of Election Infrastructure During the 2016 Election: Summary of Initial Findings and Recommendations," May 8, 2018, pp. 1-2, available at: https://www.burr.senate.gov/imo/media/doc/RussRptInstlmt1-%20ElecSec%20Findings,Recs2.pdf.

[4] U.S. Department of Homeland Security and Office of the Director of National Intelligence, "Joint Statement from the Department of Homeland Security and the Office of the Director of National Intelligence on Election Security," October 7, 2016, available at: https://www.dhs.gov/news/2016/10/07/joint-statement-department-homeland-security-and-office-director-national.

[5] In announcing the sanctions, the president stated, "Today, I have ordered a number of actions in response to the Russian government's aggressive harassment of U.S. officials and cyber operations aimed at the U.S. election. These actions follow repeated private and public warnings that we have issued to the Russian government, and are a necessary and appropriate response to efforts to harm U.S. interests in violation of established international norms of behavior." See The White House, Office of the Press Secretary, "Statement by the President on Actions in Response to Russian Malicious Cyber Activity and Harassment," December 29, 2016, available at: https://obamawhitehouse.archives.gov/the-press-office/2016/12/29/statement-president-actions-response-russian-malicious-cyber-activity.

[6] Johnson, Jeh, "Statement by Secretary Jeh Johnson on the Designation of Election Infrastructure as a Critical Infrastructure Subsector," January 6, 2017, available at: https://www.dhs.gov/news/2017/01/06/statement-secretary-johnson-designation-election-infrastructure-critical.

Critical infrastructure refers to "assets, systems, and networks, whether physical or virtual, so vital to the United States that their incapacitation or destruction would have a debilitating effect on security, national economic security, national public health or safety, or any combination thereof." See U.S. Department of Homeland Security, "What Is Critical Infrastructure?," available at: https://www.dhs.gov/what-critical-infrastructure.

Today, long-standing concerns about outdated and insecure voting systems and newer developments such as cyberattacks, the designation of election systems as critical infrastructure, and allegations of widespread voter fraud, have combined to focus attention on U.S. election systems and operations. The issues highlighted in 2016 add urgency to a careful reexamination of the conduct of elections in the United States and demonstrate a need to carefully consider tradeoffs with respect to access and cybersecurity. This report responds to the needs of this moment.

ELECTIONS IN THE UNITED STATES

Unlike other nations, the United States has no centralized, nationwide election authority. The Constitution leaves it to individual states to run and regulate elections, but Congress may make regulations that supersede state regulations on the conduct of federal contests.[7]

Motivated to make participation easier and election administration more efficient, some states have introduced new approaches to voting, such as in-person early voting, vote centers, and voting by mail. However, in an era when smart phones have become ubiquitous and the Internet plays an integral part in most people's lives, citizens must ask whether there are still further new innovative approaches to voting and consider what voting may look like in the future. Can, for example, safe and secure systems be developed to enable Internet or other remote voting in elections?

Efforts to Improve the Administration of Elections

Over the past two decades, numerous initiatives have been launched to improve U.S. election systems, with activity especially intense after the 2000 presidential election. Progress has been made since 2001, but old problems persist and new problems emerge. U.S. elections are subject to aging equipment, targeting by external actors, a lack of sustained funding, and growing expectations that voting should be more accessible, convenient, and secure. The present issues and threat environment provides an extraordinary opportunity to marshal science and technology to create more resilient and adaptive election systems that are accessible, reliable, verifiable, and secure.

Charge to the Committee

In 2016, amid concerns about the state of U.S. election infrastructure, the Carnegie Corporation of New York and the William and Flora Hewlett

---

[7] U.S. Constitution, Article I § 4.

Foundation provided support for the National Academies of Sciences, Engineering, and Medicine to consider the future of voting in the United States. In response, the National Academies appointed an ad hoc committee, the Committee on the Future of Voting: Accessible, Reliable, Verifiable Technology, to:

1. Document the current state of play in terms of technology, standards, and resources for voting technologies.
2. Examine challenges arising out of the 2016 federal election.
3. Evaluate advances in technology currently and soon-to-be available that can improve voting.
4. Offer recommendations that provide a vision of voting that is easier, accessible, reliable, and verifiable.

In carrying out its charge, the committee was mindful of the context in which its study was conducted. The committee saw its work as an opportunity to address concerns about the "hard" (e.g., all components of election systems including hardware and software) and "soft" (e.g., education and training of election workforce, law, and governance) issues associated with elections and to address new threats that could erode confidence in the results of elections. The committee recommendations articulated in this report address U.S. elections holistically, as the elections system itself is composed of numerous component systems. Issues related to voting (e.g., voter identification laws, gerrymandering, foreign and domestic disinformation, campaign financing, etc.) not addressed in this report were considered by the committee as outside its charge.

As this report illustrates, voting in the United States is a complicated process that involves multiple levels of government, personnel with a variety of skills and capabilities, and numerous electronic systems that interact in the performance of a multitude of tasks. Unfortunately, our current system is vulnerable to internal and external threats.

For this study, the committee examined the various election systems in use in the United States, the diverse parties involved in the administration of elections, research on elections, the availability of resources, and structural gaps. To create a system of voting for the future, the committee makes the following recommendations.[8]

---

[8] The initial digit in each numbered recommendation refers to the number of the chapter in this report in which the associated topic is discussed.

RECOMMENDATIONS ON COMPONENTS OF ELECTIONS

Voter Registration and Voter Registration Databases

Recommendations

4.1 Election administrators should routinely assess the integrity of voter registration databases and the integrity of voter registration databases connected to other applications. They should develop plans that detail security procedures for assessing voter registration database integrity and put in place systems that detect efforts to probe, tamper with, or interfere with voter registration systems. States should require election administrators to report any detected compromises or vulnerabilities in voter registration systems to the U.S. Department of Homeland Security, the U.S. Election Assistance Commission, and state officials.

4.2 Vendors should be required to report to their customers, the U.S. Department of Homeland Security, the U.S. Election Assistance Commission, and state officials any detected efforts to probe, tamper with, or interfere with voter registration systems.

4.3 All states should participate in a system of cross-state matching of voter registrations, such as the Electronic Registration Information Center (ERIC). States must ensure that, in the utilization of cross-matching voter databases, eligible voters are not removed from voter rolls.

4.4 Organizations engaged in managing and cross-matching voter information should continue to improve security and privacy practices. These organizations should be subject to external audits to ensure compliance with best security practices.

Voting by Mail, Including Absentee Voting

Recommendation

4.5 All voting jurisdictions should provide means for a voter to easily check whether a ballot sent by mail has been dispatched to him or her and, subsequently, whether his or her marked ballot has been received and accepted by the appropriate elections officials.

Pollbooks

Recommendations

4.6 Jurisdictions that use electronic pollbooks should have backup plans in place to provide access to current voter registration lists in the event of any disruption.

4.7 Congress should authorize and fund the National Institute of Standards and Technology, in consultation with the U.S. Election Assistance Commission, to develop security standards and verification and validation protocols for electronic pollbooks in addition to the standards and verification and validation protocols they have developed for voting systems.

4.8 Election administrators should routinely assess the security of electronic pollbooks against a range of threats such as threats to the integrity, confidentiality, or availability of pollbooks. They should develop plans that detail security procedures for assessing electronic pollbook integrity.

Ballot Design

Recommendation

4.9 State requirements for ballot design (inclusive of print, screen, audio, etc.) and testing should use best practices developed by the U.S. Election Assistance Commission and other organizations with expertise in voter usability design (such as the Center for Civic Design).

Voting Technology

Recommendations

4.10 States and local jurisdictions should have policies in place for routine replacement of election systems.

4.11 Elections should be conducted with human-readable paper ballots. These may be marked by hand or by machine (using a ballot-marking device); they may be counted by hand or by machine (using an optical scanner).[9] Recounts and audits should be conducted by human inspection of the human-readable por-

---

[9] A modern form of optical scanner, a *digital scanner*, captures, interprets, and stores a high-resolution image of the voter's ballot at a resolution of 300 dots per inch (DPI) or higher.

tion of the paper ballots. Voting machines that do not provide the capacity for independent auditing (e.g., machines that do not produce a voter-verifiable paper audit trail) should be removed from service as soon as possible.

4.12 Every effort should be made to use human-readable paper ballots in the 2018 federal election. All local, state, and federal elections should be conducted using human-readable paper ballots by the 2020 presidential election.

4.13 Computers and software used to prepare ballots (i.e., ballot-marking devices) should be separate from computers and software used to count and tabulate ballots (scanners). Voters should have an opportunity to review and confirm their selections before depositing the ballot for tabulation.[10]

Voting System Certification

Recommendations

4.14 If the principles and guidelines of the final Voluntary Voting System Guidelines are consistent with those proposed in September 2017, they should be adopted by the U.S. Election Assistance Commission.

4.15 Congress should:

  a. authorize and fund the U.S. Election Assistance Commission to develop voluntary certification standards for voter registration databases, electronic pollbooks, chain-of-custody procedures, and auditing; and

  b. provide the funding necessary to sustain the U.S. Election Assistance Commission's Voluntary Voting System Guidelines standard-setting process and certification program.

4.16 The U.S. Election Assistance Commission and the National Institute of Standards and Technology should continue the process of refining and improving the Voluntary Voting System Guidelines to reflect changes in how elections are administered, to respond to new challenges to election systems (e.g., cyberattacks), and to take advantage of opportunities as new technologies become available.

---

[10] Throughout this report, to be *counted* means to be included in a vote tally. *Tally* refers to the total number of votes cast. *Tabulation* refers to the aggregation of the votes cast by individual voters to produce vote totals.

4.17 Strong cybersecurity standards should be incorporated into the standards-setting and certification processes at the federal and state levels.

RECOMMENDATIONS ON ENSURING
THE INTEGRITY OF ELECTIONS

Election Cybersecurity

Recommendations

5.1 Election systems should continue to be considered as U.S. Department of Homeland Security-designated critical infrastructure.

5.2 The U.S. Election Assistance Commission and U.S. Department of Homeland Security should continue to develop and maintain a detailed set of cybersecurity best practices for state and local election officials. Election system vendors and state and local election officials should incorporate these best practices into their operations.

5.3 The U.S. Election Assistance Commission should closely monitor the expenditure of funds made available to the states for election security through the 2018 omnibus appropriations bill to ensure that the funds enhance security practices and do not simply replace local dollars with federal support for ongoing activities.[11] The U.S. Election Assistance Commission should closely monitor any future federal funding designated to enhance election security.

5.4 Congress should provide funding for state and local governments to improve their cybersecurity capabilities on an ongoing basis.

Election Auditing

Recommendations

5.5 Each state should require a comprehensive system of post-election audits of processes and outcomes. These audits should be conducted by election officials in a transparent manner, with as much observation by the public as is feasible, up to limits imposed to ensure voter privacy.

5.6 Jurisdictions should conduct audits of voting technology and processes (for voter registration, ballot preparation, voting, election

---

[11] See H.R. 1625 - Consolidated Appropriations Act, 2018, Section 501, available at: https://www.congress.gov/bill/115th-congress/house-bill/1625/text.

reporting, etc.) after each election. Privacy-protected audit data should be made publicly available to permit others to replicate audit results.

5.7 Audits of election outcomes should include manual examination of statistically appropriate samples of paper ballots cast.

5.8 States should mandate risk-limiting audits prior to the certification of election results.[12] With current technology, this requires the use of paper ballots. States and local jurisdictions should implement risk-limiting audits within a decade. They should begin with pilot programs and work toward full implementation. Risk-limiting audits should be conducted for all federal and state election contests, and for local contests where feasible.

5.9 State and local jurisdictions purchasing election systems should ensure that the systems will support cost-effective risk-limiting audits.

5.10 State and local jurisdictions should conduct and assess pilots of end-to-end-verifiable election systems in elections using paper ballots.

Internet Voting

Recommendations

5.11 At the present time, the Internet (or any network connected to the Internet) should not be used for the return of marked ballots.[13,14] Further, Internet voting should not be used in the future until and unless very robust guarantees of security and verifiability are developed and in place, as no known technology guarantees the secrecy, security, and verifiability of a marked ballot transmitted over the Internet.[15]

5.12 U.S. Election Assistance Commission standards and state laws should be revised to support pilot programs to explore and validate new election technologies and practices. Election officials are encouraged to seek expert and public comment on proposed new election technology before it is piloted.

---

[12] Risk-limiting audits examine individual randomly selected paper ballots until there is sufficient statistical assurance to demonstrate that the chance that an incorrect reported outcome escaping detection and correction is less than a predetermined risk limit.

[13] Inclusive of transmission via email or fax or via phone lines.

[14] The Internet is an acceptable medium for the transmission of unmarked ballots to voters so long as voter privacy is maintained and the integrity of the received ballot is protected.

[15] If secure Internet voting becomes feasible and is adopted, alternative ballot casting options should be made available to those individuals who do not have sufficient access to the Internet.

RECOMMENDATIONS ON SYSTEMIC ISSUES

Election Administrator and Poll Worker Training

Recommendations

6.1 Congress should provide adequate funding for the U.S. Election Assistance Commission to continue to serve as a national clearinghouse of information on election administration.

6.2 The U.S. Election Assistance Commission, with assistance from the national associations of state and local election administrators, should encourage, develop, and enhance information technology training programs to educate state and local technical staff on effective election administration.

6.3 Universities and community colleges should increase efforts to design curricula that address the growing organizational management and information technology needs of the election community.

The Voting Technology Marketplace

Recommendations

6.4 Congress should:
a. create incentive programs for public-private partnerships to develop modern election technology;
b. appropriate funds for distribution by the U.S. Election Assistance Commission for the ongoing modernization of election systems; and
c. authorize and appropriate funds to the National Institute of Standards and Technology to establish Common Data Formats for auditing, voter registration, and other election systems.

6.5 Along with Congress, states should allocate funds for the modernization of election systems.

6.6 The U.S. Election Assistance Commission and the National Institute of Standards and Technology should continue to collaborate on changes to the certification process that encourage the modernization of voting systems.

6.7 The National Institute of Standards and Technology should complete the Common Data Format standard for election systems.

6.8 New election systems should conform to the Common Data Format standard developed by the National Institute of Standards and Technology.

The Federal Role

Recommendation

6.9 To improve the overall performance of the election process:
   a. The president should nominate and Congress should confirm a full U.S. Election Assistance Commission and ensure that the U.S. Election Assistance Commission has sufficient members to sustain a quorum.
   b. Congress should fully fund the U.S. Election Assistance Commission to carry out its existing functions.
   c. Congress should require state and local election officials to provide the U.S. Election Assistance Commission with data on voting system failures during elections as well as information on other difficulties arising during elections (e.g., long lines, fraudulent voting, intrusions into voter registration databases, etc.). This information should be publicly available.

RECOMMENDATIONS ON SECURING THE FUTURE OF VOTING

7.1 Congress should provide appropriate funding to the U.S. Election Assistance Commission to carry out the functions assigned to it in the Help America Vote Act of 2002 as well as those articulated in this report.

7.2 Congress should authorize and provide appropriate funding to the National Institute of Standards and Technology to carry out its current elections-related functions and to perform the additional functions articulated in this report.

7.3 Congress should authorize and fund immediately a major initiative on voting that supports basic, applied, and translational research relevant to the administration, conduct, and performance of elections. This initiative should include academic centers to foster collaboration both across disciplines and with state and local election officials and industry.

The U.S. Election Assistance Commission, National Institute of Standards and Technology, U.S. Department of Homeland Security, National Science Foundation, and U.S. Department of Defense should sponsor research to:
- determine means for providing voters with the ability to easily check whether a ballot sent by mail has been dispatched to him or her and, subsequently, whether his or her marked ballot has been received and accepted by the appropriate elections officials;

- evaluate the reliability of various approaches (e.g., signature, biometric, etc.) to voter authentication;
- explore options for testing the usability and comprehensibility of ballot designs created within tight, pre-election timeframes;
- understand the effects of coercion, vote buying, theft, etc., especially among disadvantaged groups, on voting by mail and to devise technologies for reducing this threat;
- determine voter practices regarding the verification of ballot marking device–generated ballots and the likelihood that voters, both with and without disabilities, will recognize errors or omissions;
- assess the potential benefits and risks of Internet voting;
- evaluate end-to-end-verifiable election systems in various election scenarios and assess the potential utility of such systems for Internet voting; and
- address any other issues that arise concerning the integrity of U.S. elections.

CONCLUSION

As a nation, we have the capacity to build an elections system for the future, but doing so requires focused attention from citizens, federal, state, and local governments, election administrators, and innovators in academia and industry. It also requires a commitment of appropriate resources. Representative democracy only works if all eligible citizens can participate in elections, have their ballots accurately cast, counted, and tabulated, and be confident that their ballots have been accurately cast, counted, and tabulated.

1

Introduction

"The right to vote freely for the candidate of one's choice is of the essence of a democratic society . . ."[1]

"Every voter's vote is entitled to be counted once. It must be correctly counted and reported."[2]

During the 2016 presidential election, America's election infrastructure was targeted by a foreign government.[3] According to assessments by members of the U.S. Intelligence Community,[4] actors sponsored by the Russian government "obtained and maintained access to elements of multiple US state or local electoral boards."[5] While the full

---

[1] *Reynolds v. Sims*, 377 U.S. 533 (1964).

[2] *Gray v. Sanders*, 372 U.S. 368 (1963).
Throughout this report, to be *counted* means to be included in a vote tally. *Tally* refers to the total number of votes cast. *Tabulation* refers to the aggregation of the votes cast by individual voters to produce vote totals.

[3] For the purposes of this report, *election infrastructure* is defined as the physical and organizational structures and facilities and personnel needed for the operation of elections.

[4] The U.S. Intelligence Community consists of 16 agencies working under the coordination of the Office of the Director of National Intelligence. The 16 agencies are the: Central Intelligence Agency; Defense Intelligence Agency; Federal Bureau of Investigation; National Geospatial-Intelligence Agency; National Reconnaissance Office; National Security Agency/Central Security Service; U.S. Department of Energy; U.S. Department of Homeland Security (DHS); U.S. Department of State; U.S. Department of the Treasury; Drug Enforcement Administration; U.S. Air Force; U.S. Army; U.S. Coast Guard; U.S. Marine Corps; and U.S. Navy.

[5] The U.S. Department of Homeland Security (DHS) assessed "that the types of systems Russian actors targeted or compromised were not involved in vote tallying." See Office of the

extent and impact of these activities is not known and our understanding of these events is evolving, there is little doubt that these efforts represented an assault on the American system of representative democracy. The 2016 Russian probes of the U.S. voting infrastructure also were accompanied by directed social media campaigns spreading disinformation that sought to divide the American electorate and undermine confidence in democratic institutions. As former Central Intelligence Agency and National Security Agency Director Michael Hayden observed in testimony to the committee that authored this report, these efforts represented part of a sustained campaign to discredit Western countries and institutions and specifically "Western democratic processes and the American election."[6] The Russian campaign represents an unsettling development that adds greatly to the technical and operational challenges facing election administrators.

The vulnerability of election systems to cyberattacks became a growing concern during the campaign leading up to the 2016 presidential election.[7] That threat caused so much concern that, in the fall of 2016, the federal

---

Director of National Intelligence, "Assessing Russian Activities and Intentions in Recent US Elections, Intelligence Community Assessment," January 6, 2017, p. iii, available at: https://www.dni.gov/files/documents/ICA_2017_01.pdf. Bolded text is original to the document.

By September 2017, voter registration systems or public election sites in 21 states had been identified by DHS as having been targeted by Russian hackers. See, e.g., National Association of Secretaries of State, "NASS Statement on US Department of Homeland Security (DHS) Outreach to 21 States Regarding Potential Targeting," September 25, 2017, available at: https://www.nass.org/node/284 and Horwitz, Sari, Ellen Nakashima, and Matea Gold, "DHS Tells States About Russian Hacking During 2016 Election," *Washington Post*, September 22, 2017.

Voter registration systems and public election websites (e.g., state "my voter" pages) are *election systems*. For the purposes of this report, election system is defined as a technology-based system that is used to collect, process, and store data related to elections and election administration. In addition to voter registration systems and public election websites, election systems include voting systems (the means through which voters cast their ballots), vote tabulation systems, election night reporting systems, and auditing systems.

Whether there were attacks on voting systems or vote tabulation systems is unknown. The committee authoring this report is not aware of an ongoing investigation into this possibility. In 2016, gaps in intelligence gathering, information sharing, and reporting led to problems that were underappreciated at the time of the intrusions leaving considerable uncertainty about what happened, even today. See, e.g., U.S. Senate Select Committee on Intelligence, "Russian Targeting of Election Infrastructure During the 2016 Election: Summary of Initial Findings and Recommendations," May 8, 2018, pp. 1-2, available at: https://www.burr.senate.gov/imo/media/doc/RussRptInstlmt1-%20ElecSec%20Findings,Recs2.pdf.

[6] Comments by General Michael Hayden at the third meeting of the Committee on the Future of Voting, the National Academies, October 18, 2017, Washington, DC, webcast available at: https://livestream.com/accounts/7036396/events/7752647.

[7] By late fall 2016, the U.S. intelligence community had determined that Russia had directed the theft and disclosure of emails from U.S. persons and institutions, including U.S. political organizations, for the purpose of "interfer[ing] with the US election process." See U.S. Department of Homeland Security and Office of the Director of National Intelligence, "Joint Statement from the Department of Homeland Security and the Office of the Director of National Intelligence

government took the unusual step of issuing a joint statement from the U.S. Department of Homeland Security (DHS) and the Office of the Director of National Intelligence (ODNI) urging state and local governments to be "vigilant and seek cybersecurity assistance from DHS."[8] In late December 2016, as the extent of Russian activities became apparent, President Barack Obama invoked sanctions against Russia for its efforts to disrupt the presidential election. In early January 2017, then-DHS Secretary Jeh Johnson observed that, "Given the vital role elections play in this country, it is clear that certain systems and assets of election infrastructure meet the definition of critical infrastructure, in fact and in law." In early 2017, the nation's election systems were given critical infrastructure status.[9]

Since the 2000 election, election infrastructure has been a focus of attention due to concerns about aging and insecure voting equipment, inadequate poll worker training, insufficient numbers of voting machines and pollbooks, deficient voter registration information systems, and inadequate verification procedures for votes cast. Long before concerns about Russian interference surfaced, state and local election administrators had been forced to reevaluate and modernize the operation of voting systems[10] in the wake of incidents such as the "hanging chad" debacle in the 2000 presidential election and long lines that occurred in some jurisdictions in the 2004, 2008, and 2012 elections. In advance of the 2016 election, as they had in the past, officials worked aggressively to ensure that the 2016 national election would run smoothly and without disruptions and that election systems—including public election websites, voter registration systems, voting systems, vote tabulation systems, election night reporting systems, and auditing systems—would meet the challenges of a national election.

Today, long-standing concerns about outdated and insecure voting systems and newer developments such as cyberattacks, the designation of election systems as critical infrastructure, and allegations of widespread voter fraud, have combined to focus attention on U.S. election systems

---

on Election Security," October 7, 2016, available at: https://www.dhs.gov/news/2016/10/07/joint-statement-department-homeland-security-and-office-director-national.

[8] "Joint Statement from the Department of Homeland Security and the Office of the Director of National Intelligence on Election Security."

Critical infrastructure refers to "assets, systems, and networks, whether physical or virtual, so vital to the United States that their incapacitation or destruction would have a debilitating effect on security, national economic security, national public health or safety, or any combination thereof." See U.S. Department of Homeland Security, "What Is Critical Infrastructure?," available at: https://www.dhs.gov/what-critical-infrastructure.

[9] Johnson, Jeh, "Statement by Secretary Jeh Johnson on the Designation of Election Infrastructure as a Critical Infrastructure Subsector," January 6, 2017, available at: https://www.dhs.gov/news/2017/01/06/statement-secretary-johnson-designation-election-infrastructure-critical.

[10] Throughout this report, the term *voting system* refers to the means through which voters cast their ballots.

and operations. The issues highlighted in 2016 add urgency to a careful reexamination of the conduct of elections in the United States and demonstrate a need to carefully consider tradeoffs with respect to access and cybersecurity. This report responds to the needs of this moment.

ELECTIONS IN THE UNITED STATES

Unlike other nations, the United States has no centralized, nationwide election authority.[11] The Constitution leaves it to individual states to run and regulate elections (see Box 1-1).[12] Congress may, however, make regulations that supersede state regulations on the conduct of federal contests. Federal anti-discrimination laws have been enacted to ensure registration and poll access for all eligible voters.[13]

Until the Australian (secret) ballot was adopted by most of the states in the 1890s, many Americans voted in public, sometimes casting their votes orally, with no voting booths or other means of protecting the confidentiality of an individual's vote.[14] (See Figure 1-1.)

---

[11] Decentralization allows voting technologies to be adapted to meet local needs, laws, and traditions. It may spur innovation, with states serving as, in the words of U.S. Supreme Court Justice Louis Brandeis, "laboratories of democracy." Decentralization may also help impede certain attacks on election infrastructure, as it greatly multiplies potential points of attack.

Decentralization implies, however, that there will be a diversity of strength and weakness, and malicious actors have the freedom to focus on the most weakly defended systems. In a close election, successful attacks against a few weakly protected swing states or swing districts could tip national results. Moreover, a successful attack anywhere will detract from voter confidence everywhere.

States and localities often lack the resources that a central government might bring to support of election infrastructure.

Decentralization also fragments the markets for election technologies. This might affect costs and hinder innovation.

The diffuse responsibility for American elections can also contribute to a lack of clarity with regard to the level of government that is responsible for responding to acute attacks on election infrastructure.

[12] In some states and jurisdictions, the conduct of elections and the registration of voters are administered by two separate and distinct entities.

[13] See U.S. Constitution, Article I § 4 and 4th, 15th, 19th, 24th, and 26th Amendments to the U.S. Constitution; Voting Rights Act, 52 U.S.C. §§ 10101 et seq.; Voting Age Act, 52 U.S.C. §§ 10701 and 10702; Voting Accessibility for Elderly and Handicapped Act, 52 U.S.C. §§ 20101 et seq.; Uniformed and Overseas Citizens Absentee Voting Act, 52 U.S.C. §§ 20301 et seq.; and National Voter Registration Act, 52 U.S.C. §§ 20501 et seq.

[14] See Ludington, Arthur C., American Ballot Laws, 1888–1910. New York State Education Department Bulletin No. 448 (Albany: University of the State of New York, 1911); Evans, Eldon Cobb, A History of the Australian Ballot System in the United States (Chicago: University of Chicago Press, 1917); and Katz, Jonathan N. and Brian R. Sala, "Careerism, Committee Assignments, and the Electoral Connection," American Political Science Review, 1996, No. 90, pp. 21-33, Table 1.

BOX 1-1
Election Management and the U.S. Constitution

The U.S. Constitution as originally ratified is silent about who can vote. Suffrage requirements were left to the states, which until 1828 generally restricted voting to white male property owners. The Constitution grants Congress the authority to make regulations that supersede state laws and regulations pertaining to congressional elections.

Over time, by law and custom, each state has devised and periodically revised its own election procedures. Many procedures are reflected in local laws. Every state has a chief election official who has oversight responsibility for elections in the state. For about half of the states, this is an elected secretary of state. Other states have other leadership models (e.g., appointed secretaries of state, lieutenant governors, and election boards).

The particular voting systems used to cast ballots are chosen independently by the states, often by local governments. The federal government, through the Election Assistance Commission, helps to develop standards that guide the development of voting systems, but these standards are voluntary—states are free to adopt or ignore them. Decisions regarding the design of (and support for) other election systems are likewise the prerogative of the individual states.

Today, U.S. elections are administered by thousands of jurisdictions. Elections encompass both highly visible contests, such as the presidential election, and contests to elect minor local officials. Some jurisdictions contain fewer than 100 voters while others contain millions. Elections are overseen by state and/or local officials acting according to laws and rules promulgated by state and local governments. Many elections offices have few dedicated staff and little access to the latest information technology (IT) training or tools.[15] While elections end for most voters once they have cast their ballots and the results of the election are announced, election administrators must constantly be planning for future elections.

Motivated to make participation easier and election administration more efficient, some states have introduced new modes of voting, such as in-person early voting, vote centers, and voting by mail. Estimates are difficult to make with available data, but in the 2016 presidential election, it appears that between 55 and 60 million of 138.8 million of those who

---

[15] Kimball, David C., and Brady Baybeck, "Are All Jurisdictions Equal? Size Disparity in Election Administration," *Election Law Journal*, 2013, No. 12, pp. 130-145.

FIGURE 1-1 George Caleb Bingham, American, 1811–1879; *The County Election*, 1852; oil on canvas; 38 × 52 inches; Saint Louis Art Museum, Gift of Bank of America 44:2001. Image courtesy Saint Louis Art Museum.
Bingham's painting depicts the chaotic and public nature of voting in the 19th century. Voters often approached an election official to vote by voice while politicians stood close by to watch and influence voters. Nearby, sometimes libations awaited those who had cast the "right vote."

voted took advantage of these emerging approaches.[16] However, in an era when smart phones have become ubiquitous and the Internet plays an integral part in most people's lives, citizens must ask whether there are still further new innovative approaches to voting and consider what voting may look like in the future. Can, for example, safe and secure systems be developed to enable Internet or other remote voting in elections?

---

[16] Estimates of the number of voters who used various voting modes are imprecise because states do not uniformly report turnout by voting mode. These estimates are derived from two sources, respectively: U.S. Census Bureau, "Current Population Survey, Voting and Registration Supplement," 2016 and U.S. Election Assistance Commission, "2016 Election Administration and Voting Survey" (EAVS), June 29, 2016.

EFFORTS TO IMPROVE THE ADMINISTRATION OF ELECTIONS

Over the past two decades, numerous initiatives have been launched to improve U.S. election systems, with activity especially intense after the 2000 presidential election. Two national bipartisan commissions, the National Commission on Federal Election Reform and the Commission on Federal Election Reform, followed a long-standing tradition of assembling panels of notable politicians, academics, and public intellectuals to study national crises and propose reforms. The National Commission on Federal Election Reform, which conducted its work in 2001, was chaired by former Presidents Gerald Ford and Jimmy Carter.[17] The report of the Ford-Carter Commission, titled "To Assure Pride and Confidence in the Electoral Process," issued several recommendations concerning voter registration, election systems, and election operations. These recommendations informed the Help America Vote Act (HAVA) (see below) passed in 2002.[18,19] The Commission on Federal Election Reform, chaired by President Carter and former-Secretary of State James Baker, conducted its work from 2004 to 2005. Its report, "Building Confidence in U.S. Elections," looked beyond HAVA to provide recommendations related to voter registration, voter identification, improved security for elections (including voter-verifiable paper trails), and independent, professional election administration.[20]

Universities have contributed to sustained efforts to build a research-based infrastructure aimed at improving the administration of elections on a scientific and technical basis. Noting a "distressing lack of previous research" on voting that had led to the use of technologies that were "unreliable and inaccurate," the Caltech/MIT Voting Technology Project (VTP) was established in December 2000 to develop voting systems standards and testing practices on a foundation of scientific and engineering research. Over time, VTP has created a body of research and facilitated new collaborations with state and local election administrators to improve voting systems and the voting experience.[21] Other current university-based programs include the Center for Voting Technology Research at the Univer-

---

[17] See https://millercenter.org/issues-policy/governance/the-national-commission-on-federal-election-reform.

[18] The National Commission on Federal Election Reform, "To Assure Pride and Confidence in the Electoral Process," 2001, available at: http://web1.millercenter.org/commissions/comm_2001.pdf.

[19] Help America Vote Act of 2002 (Pub.L. 107–252).

[20] Commission on Federal Election Reform, "Building Confidence in U.S. Elections," 2005, available at: https://www.eac.gov/assets/1/6/Exhibit%20M.PDF.

[21] See https://vote.caltech.edu.

sity of Connecticut[22] and the Voting System Technical Oversight Program at Ball State University.[23]

HAVA created the U.S. Election Assistance Commission (EAC), an independent bipartisan federal agency, to serve as a clearinghouse for election administration research and information and to disburse federal funds to states for the replacement of antiquated voting systems and the improvement of election administration; mandated that states create centralized, computerized voting registration systems; and required minimal standards for federal elections.[24] In order to facilitate the modernization of election technologies, HAVA authorized a $3 billion appropriation for the purchase of new voting systems. HAVA also gave the National Institute for Standards and Technology (NIST) a key role in improving election infrastructure through, for example, the development of voluntary voting system guidelines.

In March 2013, the bipartisan Presidential Commission on Election Administration was established by President Obama to

> identify best practices and otherwise make recommendations to promote the efficient administration of elections in order to ensure that all eligible voters have the opportunity to cast their ballots without undue delay, and to improve the experience of voters facing other obstacles in casting their ballots, such as members of the military, overseas voters, voters with disabilities, and voters with limited English proficiency.[25]

The commission's resulting report, "The American Voting Experience," warned of a new "impending crisis in voting technology" as the voting

---

[22] See https://voter.engr.uconn.edu/voter/.

[23] See http://bowencenterforpublicaffairs.org/institutes/policy-research/election-admin/vstop.

[24] The EAC's "four commissioners are nominated by the President on recommendations from the majority and minority leadership in the U.S. House of Representatives and the U.S. Senate. No more than two commissioners may belong to the same political party. Once confirmed by the full Senate, commissioners may serve two consecutive terms." See U.S. Election Assistance Commission, "About U.S. EAC: Commissioners," available at: https://www.eac.gov/about/commissioners/.

There are currently two vacancies on the commission. Any action of the commission authorized by HAVA requires approval of at least three of its members. See HAVA 42 U.S.C. § 15328.

[25] The White House, "Executive Order – Establishment of the Presidential Commission on Election Administration," March 23, 2013, available at: https://obamawhitehouse.archives.gov/the-press-office/2013/03/28/executive-order-establishment-presidential-commission-election-administr.

systems developed and installed in the early 2000s began to wear out and fail. [26]

At the state level, election administrators have been collaborating with academic researchers, NIST,[27] and the EAC on experiments to improve ballot design; improve polling place accessibility; develop language assistance resources; expand the use of voting by mail; operate vote centers; improve voter experience in polling places; and conduct audits to test the security of voting systems.

While progress has been made since 2001, old problems persist and new problems emerge. U.S. elections are subject to aging equipment, targeting by external actors, a lack of sustained funding, and growing expectations that voting should be more accessible, convenient, and secure. The present issues and threat environment provide an extraordinary opportunity to marshal science and technology to create more resilient and adaptive election systems that are accessible, reliable, verifiable, and secure.

CHARGE TO THE COMMITTEE

In 2016, amid concerns about the state of U.S. election infrastructure, the Carnegie Corporation of New York and the William and Flora Hewlett Foundation provided support for the National Academies of Sciences, Engineering, and Medicine to consider the future of the voting in the United States. In response, the National Academies appointed an ad hoc committee, the Committee on the Future of Voting: Accessible, Reliable, Verifiable Technology, to:

1. Document the current state of play in terms of technology, standards, and resources for voting technologies.
2. Examine challenges arising out of the 2016 federal election.
3. Evaluate advances in technology currently and soon-to-be available that can improve voting.
4. Offer recommendations that provide a vision of voting that is easier, accessible, reliable, and verifiable.

In carrying out its charge, the committee was mindful of the context in

---

[26] Presidential Commission on Election Administration, "The American Voting Experience: Report and Recommendations of the Presidential Commission on Election Administration," January 2014, available at: https://www.eac.gov/assets/1/6/Amer-Voting-Exper-final-draft-01-09-14-508.pdf, p. 4.

The report offered recommendations to address this "impending crisis" but also voter registration, access to the polls, and polling place management.

[27] NIST often carries out its work in collaboration with researchers, election administrators, vendors, and the U.S. Election Assistance Commission.

which its study was conducted. The committee saw its work as an opportunity to address concerns about the "hard" (e.g., all components of election systems including hardware and software) and "soft" (e.g., education and training of election workforce, law, and governance) issues associated with elections and to address new threats that could erode confidence in the results of elections. The committee recommendations articulated in Chapters 4, 5, 6, and 7 address U.S. elections holistically, as the elections system is compromised of numerous component systems. Issues related to voting (e.g., voter identification laws, gerrymandering, foreign and domestic disinformation, campaign financing, etc.) not addressed in this report were considered by the committee as outside its charge.

Over the course of this study, the committee reviewed extensive background materials. It held six meetings where invited experts spoke to the committee about a range of topics including voter registration, voting accessibility, voting technologies and market impediments to technological innovation, cybersecurity, post-election audits, and the education and training of election workers. Agendas for the committee's meetings appear in Appendix B. The committee did not access classified information but instead relied on information in the public domain, including state and federal government reports, published academic literature, testimony from congressional hearings, and presentations to the committee.

ORGANIZATION OF THE REPORT

Chapter 2 provides an overview of issues arising in the 2016 election. Chapter 3 provides an overview of U.S. election systems. Chapters 4, 5, and 6 describe challenges for election administration and provide the committee's findings and recommendations. Chapter 7 offers the committee's conclusions about securing the future of voting and offers concluding recommendations.

2

Voting and the 2016 Presidential Election

Federal elections are an enormous undertaking. There are thousands of election administration jurisdictions in the United States, and in the 2016 presidential election, there were 178,217 individual precincts[1] and 116,990 physical Election Day polling places.[2,3] Election administration jurisdictions operated more than 8,500 locations where ballots could be cast prior to Election Day.[4]

Greater than 60 percent of the U.S. voting-eligible population (138.8 million voters out of 230.6 million eligible Americans) cast ballots in the 2016 presidential election.[5] Voter turnout exceeded 70 percent in four

---

[1] An individual precinct is a geographic voting area to which individuals are assigned and that determine the ballot type voters receive.

[2] A polling place is the location where one can vote on Election Day.

[3] "2016 Election Administration and Voting Survey" (EAVS), p.13. Statistics quoted in this report that rely on the EAVS reflect answers from jurisdictions that provided information to the EAC and totals, therefore, may not add up to 100 percent. The EAVS contains the most comprehensive nationwide data about election administration in the United States. It includes responses from all 50 states, the District of Columbia, and four U.S. territories. The U.S. Election Assistance Commission (EAC) administers the survey to meet its obligations under the Help America Vote Act of 2002 to serve as a national clearinghouse and resource for the compilation of information related to federal elections. Data are collected at the local level by counties or the county equivalent and include information related to voter registration; military and overseas voters; early and by mail voting; provisional voting; voter participation; voting equipment usage; and poll workers, polling places, and precincts.

[4] Ibid.

[5] See United States Election Project, "2016 November General Election Turnout Rates," available at: http://www.electproject.org/2016g.

states.[6] Greater than 41 percent of all ballots were cast before Election Day; of these, approximately 17 percent were cast using in-person early voting while nearly 24 percent were cast by mail.[7] While rates of voting by mail vary significantly across the country, nationally approximately 80 percent of ballots transmitted to voters were returned. In most states, greater than 90 percent of returned ballots met eligibility requirements and were counted.[8]

ISSUES ARISING IN THE 2016 PRESIDENTIAL ELECTION

During the 2016 election, the media and citizen groups who monitor the voting process reported problems experienced at the polls, such as confusion over state requirements regarding voter identification, difficulties with polling place procedures, and faulty voting equipment. However, in responses to the "Survey of the Performance of the American Electorate," the only large-scale academic survey devoted to election administration topics, the vast majority of voters reported that they did not encounter problems at the polls or when voting by mail.[9] This does not mean that there were not problems that occurred unbeknownst to the voter. If an electronic voting machine, for example, were to change a vote after a voter had completed the voting process, the voter would be unaware of the problem and have no reason to report dissatisfaction.

In general, responses to the survey were similar to those given following the 2008 and 2012 elections. The only common problem reported in 2016 was long lines in some locations. However, the average wait times reported in 2016 were significantly less than those reported in 2012, when the issue was elevated to national prominence.

The 2016 election was distinguished by two notable developments: (1) the targeting of many states' voter registration systems and public election websites by Russian actors; and (2) assertions by the new president that millions of individuals voted illegally. In addition, the Russian government made efforts to influence the outcome of the election through a disinformation campaign using social media and other tactics (see Appendix C).

---

[6] Ibid. The four states were Colorado, Maine, Minnesota, and New Hampshire.
[7] Ibid, p. 8.
[8] Ibid, p. i.
[9] Stewart, Charles III. "2016 Survey of the Performance of American Elections: Final Report," 2017, available at: http://dx.doi.org/10.7910/DVN/Y38VIQ. Dr. Stewart is a member of the committee that authored the current report.

Foreign Targeting of Election Systems

In the summer of 2016, as election administrators were preparing for the upcoming presidential election, they were notified by then-Secretary of the U.S. Department of Homeland Security (DHS) Jeh Johnson of growing evidence of foreign intrusions into state election systems and of the possibility of foreign interference. In June, federal cybersecurity experts noticed that the network credentials of an Arizona county elections worker, which would allow access to Arizona's state voter registration system, had been posted on a site frequented by suspected Russian hackers. Several weeks later, Illinois Board of Elections' information technology staff noticed a significant increase in activity involving their voter registration system: "Malicious queries were hitting […the voter registration system] 5 times per second, 24 hours a day, looking for a way to break in."[10] Illinois officials took the website offline and discovered that the attack had originated overseas and had begun weeks earlier.

In October 2016, DHS and the Office of the Director of National Intelligence (ODNI) issued a joint statement on election security. The statement said that some states had seen scanning and probing of their election systems, "which in most cases originated from servers operated by a Russian company."[11] DHS urged election administrators to remain vigilant.

By late December 2016, the federal government, through a Joint Analysis Report, provided further details about Russian cyber-attacks that had targeted one of the political party's campaigns.[12] In response, President Obama expelled 35 Russian diplomats from the United States and imposed sanctions on two Russian intelligence services. The president declared that, "All Americans should be alarmed by Russia's actions," and said that his actions were "a necessary and appropriate response to efforts to harm U.S. interests in violation of established international norms of behavior."[13]

In January 2017, ODNI issued a report, "Assessing Russian Activities and Intentions in Recent US Elections." The report documented Russia's use of cyber tools and media campaigns to influence the 2016 U.S. presidential

---

[10] Fessler, Pam, "Timeline: Foreign Efforts to Hack State Election Systems and How Officials Responded," National Public Radio, July 31, 2017.

[11] "Joint Statement from the Department of Homeland Security and Office of the Director of National Intelligence on Election Security."

[12] U.S. Department of Homeland Security and Federal Bureau of Investigation, "GRIZZLY STEPPE – Russian Malicious Cyber Activity," Joint Analysis Report JAR-16-20296A, December 29, 2016, available at: https://www.us-cert.gov/sites/default/files/publications/JAR_16-20296A_GRIZZLY%20STEPPE-2016-1229.pdf.

[13] The White House. Office of the Press Secretary, "Statement by the President on Actions in Response to Russian Malicious Cyber Activity and Harassment," December 29, 2016. https://obamawhitehouse.archives.gov/the-press-office/2016/12/29/statement-president-actions-response-russian-malicious-cyber-activity.

election. Although the report primarily covered influence operations aimed at the political campaigns, it also addressed efforts to gain access to technologies associated with administering elections. It stated that:

> Russian intelligence obtained and maintained access to elements of multiple US state or local electoral boards. **DHS assesses that the types of systems Russian actors targeted or compromised were not involved in vote tallying. . . . We assess Moscow will apply lessons learned from its Putin-ordered campaign aimed at the US presidential election to future influence efforts worldwide, including against US allies and their election processes.**[14]

In early January 2017 Secretary Johnson designated the nation's election infrastructure as a subsector of the nation's critical infrastructure, stating,

> I have determined that election infrastructure in this country should be designated as a subsector of the existing Government Facilities critical infrastructure sector. Given the vital role elections play in this country, it is clear that certain systems and assets of election infrastructure meet the definition of critical infrastructure, in fact and in law.
>
> I have reached this determination so that election infrastructure will, on a more formal and enduring basis, be a priority for cybersecurity assistance and protections that the Department of Homeland Security provides to a range of private and public sector entities. By "election infrastructure," we mean storage facilities, polling places, and centralized vote tabulations locations used to support the election process, and information and communications technology to include voter registration databases, voting machines, and other systems to manage the election process and report and display results on behalf of state and local governments." [15]

By September 2017, voter registration systems or public election sites in 21 states had been identified by DHS as having been targeted by Russian hackers.[16] In May 2018, the U.S. Senate Select Committee on Intelligence released a summary of its initial findings and recommendations regarding

---

[14] Office of the Director of National Intelligence, "Assessing Russian Activities and Intentions in Recent US Elections, Intelligence Community Assessment," January 6, 2017, p. iii, available at: https://www.dni.gov/files/documents/ICA_2017_01.pdf. Bolded text is original to the document. This declassified assessment is based on a "highly classified assessment," but its conclusions are "identical to the highly classified assessment" (see p. i).

[15] See https://www.dhs.gov/news/2017/01/06/statement-secretary-johnson-designation-election-infrastructure-critical.

[16] Horwitz, Sari, Ellen Nakasmina, and Matea Gold, "DHS Tells States About Russian Hacking During 2016 Election," *Washington Post*, September 22, 2017.

the Russian targeting of election infrastructure during the 2016 election. The report states

- "In at least six states, the Russian-affiliated cyber actors went beyond scanning and conducted malicious access attempts on voting-related websites. In a small number of states, Russian-affiliated cyber actors were able to gain access to restricted elements of election infrastructure. In a small number of states, these cyber actors were in a position to, at a minimum, alter or delete voter registration data; however, they did not appear to be in a position to manipulate individual votes or aggregate vote totals." [17]
- "In addition to the cyber activity directed at state election infrastructure, Russia undertook a wide variety of intelligence-related activities targeting the U.S. voting process. These activities began at least as early as 2014, continued through Election Day 2016, and included traditional information gathering efforts as well as operations likely aimed at preparing to discredit the integrity of the U.S. voting process and election results." [18]

Assertion of Illegal Voting During the 2016 Election

Donald J. Trump won the presidency in 2016, having received a majority of electoral votes.[19,20] He did not win the popular vote, but claimed in late November 2016 that he would have won the popular vote "if you deduct the millions of people who voted illegally."[21] He repeated this claim in a January 2017 meeting with Congressional leaders, asserting that between 3 and 5 million illegal immigrants voted for Hillary Clinton.[22]

In response to the president's assertion, the bipartisan National Association of Secretaries of State (NASS) issued the following statement:

We are not aware of any evidence that supports the voter fraud claims

---

[17] U.S. Senate Select Committee on Intelligence, "Russian Targeting of Election Infrastructure During the 2016 Election: Summary of Initial Findings and Recommendations," May 8, 2018, pp. 1-2, available at: https://www.burr.senate.gov/imo/media/doc/RussRptInstlmt1-%20ElecSec%20Findings,Recs2.pdf.

[18] Ibid, p. 2.

[19] United States Congress, *Congressional Record,* Jan. 6, 2017, p. H190.

[20] President Trump received nearly 2.9 million fewer popular votes than his principal opponent, Hillary R. Clinton. Trump received 62,984,825 votes, compared to 65,863,516 for Clinton. See U.S. Federal Election Commission, "Official 2016 Presidential General Election Results," January 30, 2017, available at: https://transition.fec.gov/pubrec/fe2016/2016presgeresults.pdf.

[21] Trump, Donald, Twitter Post, November 27, 2016, 3:30 p.m., available at: https://twitter.com/realdonaldtrump/status/802972944532209664?lang=en.

[22] Shear, Michael D. and Emmarie Huetteman, "Trump Repeats Lie About Popular Vote in Meeting with Lawmakers," *New York Times,* January 23, 2017.

made by President Trump, but we are open to learning more about the Administration's concerns. In the lead up to the November 2016 election, secretaries of state expressed their confidence in the systemic integrity of our election process as a bipartisan group, and they stand behind that statement today.[23]

The committee authoring the current study did not find evidence of large-scale illegal voting in the 2016 election.

On May 11, 2017, President Trump established the Presidential Advisory Commission on Election Integrity. Vice President Mike Pence was appointed chair of the commission, and Kansas Secretary of State Kris Kobach was appointed as vice chair. The commission was asked to

> study vulnerabilities in voting systems used for federal elections that could lead to improper voter registrations, improper voting, fraudulent voter registrations, and fraudulent voting. The Commission will also study concerns about voter suppression, as well as other voting irregularities. The Commission will utilize all available data, including state and federal databases.[24]

On January 3, 2018, after two meetings of the commission, President Trump announced its disbanding.[25] The commission had been embroiled in numerous controversies, including a request for voter registration files that both Republican and Democratic state officials considered overly broad[26] and questions about whether commission proceedings complied with the Federal Advisory Committee Act and whether its own members had been excluded from deliberations.[27] The commission did not issue any reports before it was disbanded.

President Trump subsequently asked DHS to review the issue of voter fraud. When asked if DHS had plans to pursue the fraud issues, DHS spokesperson Tyler Houlton stated that the department "continues to work in support of state governments who are responsible for administering elec-

---

[23] National Association of Secretaries of State, "Jan. 24. Statement by NASS," January 24, 2017, available at: http://www.nass.org/index.php/news-releases-and-statements/release-nass-statement-election-integrity-jan17/.

[24] See https://www.whitehouse.gov/the-press-office/2017/05/11/president-announces-formation-bipartisan-presidential-commission.

[25] See https://www.whitehouse.gov/presidential-actions/executive-order-termination-presidential-advisory-commission-election-integrity/.

[26] Wines, Michael, "Asked for Voters' Data, States Give Trump Panel a Bipartisan 'No'," *New York Times*, July 1, 2017.

[27] Wines, Michael and Maggie Haberman, "Trump Closes Voter Fraud Panel That Bickered More Than It Revealed," *New York Times,* January 5, 2018.

tions, with efforts focused on securing elections against those who seek to undermine the election system or its integrity."[28]

CONCLUSION

As in previous federal elections, election administrators oversaw a complex voting process during the 2016 presidential election. Efforts by the Russian government to probe systems that help administer elections, along with related efforts to influence the election using the Internet, prompted a new awareness of additional potential vulnerabilities. The DHS designation of election infrastructure as critical national infrastructure adds an additional facet into the election process. The following chapters describe U.S. election systems and consider how developments in 2016 and 2017 and issues already associated with election infrastructure may be addressed to make voting in the future more accessible, reliable, verifiable, and secure.

---

[28] Volz, Dustin and Julia Harte, "DHS Election Unit Has No Plans for Probing U.S. Voter Fraud-Sources," *Reuters*, January 5, 2018.

3

Voting in the United States

In the United States, federal elections occur every 2 years in even-numbered years.[1] Federal regulation of elections is limited, most importantly governing voting rights and campaign finance and affecting when elections for Congress are held. The major aspects of election administration are determined by state and local laws, and elections are overseen by state and local administrators. Although local control over elections leads to variations in specific processes, elections follow the same general process throughout the country (see Figure 3-1).

During each federal election, all 435 members of the House of Representatives are elected for 2-year terms. Senators are elected for staggered 6-year terms. This means that roughly one-third of the Senate is elected every 2 years. Presidential elections are held concurrently with House and Senate elections every fourth year.

State and local contests, including ballot initiatives and referenda, often appear on the ballot alongside federal contests in even-numbered years. However, a few states hold state elections in odd-numbered years,[2] and it is common for local governments to hold elections in the spring, rather than in the fall.

Elections for most offices have a preliminary race wherein the initial field of candidates is winnowed to a smaller number. Most commonly,

---

[1] Special elections for members of Congress may be held to fill vacancies in both even and odd years.

[2] Five states, Kentucky, Louisiana, Mississippi, New Jersey, and Virginia, hold major state elections in odd-numbered years.

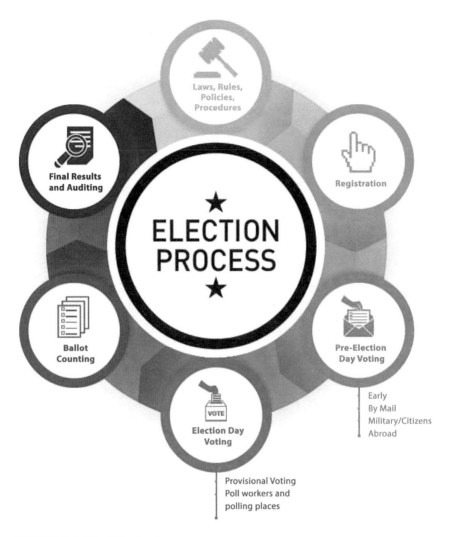

FIGURE 3-1 The U.S. election process.
SOURCE: Adapted from U.S. Election Assistance Commission, *2016 Election Administration and Voting Survey* (EAVS), June 29, 2016, p. 4. The original image, which is available at: https://www.eac.gov/assets/1/6/2016_EAVS_Comprehensive_Report. pdf, is the work of the U.S. Election Assistance Commission, taken or made during the course of an employee's official duties. As a work of the U.S. federal government, the image is in the public domain.
NOTE: This figure is provided as a general illustration of the election process. It does not include all components of the process, e.g., poll site selection.

political parties hold so-called primary elections. In primary election scenarios, candidates compete to stand as their party's single nominee in the
general election.[3] In jurisdictions that hold non-partisan elections, a first
round known as a preliminary election is held to reduce the number of
candidates prior to the general election.

The large number of elections and the numerous contests on many ballots
create an administrative challenge to election administrators. This challenge
is a principal driver for automation in American election administration.

The details of election administration vary considerably across states
and local governments. Variation exists with respect to levels of funding,[4]
human resources, how ballots are cast, and how votes are captured and
tabulated. Furthermore, federal and state laws govern how military and
overseas citizens may cast their votes in absentia.[5] The result is a diverse
and complex system of elections and wide variation in the training and
capability of election administrators and staff who administer elections.

On Election Day, problems can arise when the lines to vote are too long,
when voting rolls are inaccurate, when voting machines break down, when
ballots are poorly designed, when physical accessibility is limited, when precincts run out of ballots, when poll workers are poorly trained, or when
election systems are compromised.[6] Equipment failure, inadequate training,
or poor ballot design can lead to long wait times. Inadequate access for
voters with limited English proficiency or for voters with disabilities may be
the result of insufficient resources applied to the needs of those communities.
Inaccurate voter registration lists may stem from the absence of comprehensive and current voter registration databases. Election systems may be vulnerable to intrusions that target voter rolls or voting systems.

To ensure that the results of an election are representative of the will
of the people, every valid vote must be accurately counted. To achieve this,
eligible citizens must be able to obtain their ballots, cast their votes for their
candidates of choice, and have those votes recorded and tabulated accurately. At the same time, repeat voting and voting by ineligible individuals
must be deterred and prevented.

---

[3] In a few states, for some offices, political parties still hold conventions to nominate party
representatives in the general election.

[4] It is extremely challenging to calculate the cost of election administration in the United
States (see Appendix D).

[5] The primary federal laws affecting voting by military and overseas civilians are the Uniformed and Overseas Citizens Absentee Voting Act (UOCAVA), Pub.L. 99-410, and the Military
and Overseas Voter Empowerment Act (MOVE), Pub.L. 111-84. Both of these laws are overseen by the Federal Voting Assistance Program (FVAP), which is a part of the U.S. Department
of Defense. See https://www.fvap.gov.

[6] In addition to reliability issues and issues relating to the management of the flow of voters,
Election Day problems may include issues related to election integrity and voter privacy.

In modern elections, the voting process is largely dependent on technology-based systems known as election systems. These systems collect, process, and store data related to all aspects of election administration.[7] Election systems include public election websites (e.g., state "my voter" pages),[8] voter registration (VR) systems, voting systems (the means through which voters cast their ballots), vote tabulation systems, election night reporting systems, and auditing systems (see Figure 3-2).[9]

In the United States, votes are cast: (1) in person; (2) via mail;[10] or (3) digitally from a remote location.[11] Regardless of how a vote is cast, each voter is assigned to a voting district, typically called a precinct, which is a bounded geographic area wherein all individuals generally vote for the same set of candidates and issues. In all cases, an individual must meet eligibility requirements and, in most states, must be registered to vote before he or she may be able to cast a lawful ballot.[12]

VOTER REGISTRATION, VOTER REGISTRATION DATABASES, AND POLLBOOKS

Voter registration plays a central role in elections in 49 states and the District of Columbia,[13] as in these locations, a voter must be registered for his or her vote to count. [14] As a general rule, voters register to vote in a spe-

---

[7] King, Merle, Kennesaw State University, PowerPoint presentation to the committee (Slide 5), June 12, 2017, New York, NY. The presentation is available at: http://sites.nationalacademies. org/cs/groups/pgasite/documents/webpage/pga_180929.pdf.

[8] Georgia's My Voter Page, for instance, provides information on the state administration of elections and elections results and allows individuals to check their voter registration status, mail-in application and ballot status, and provisional ballot status; to locate poll and early voting locations; and view information about elected officials and sample ballots for upcoming elections. See https://www.mvp.sos.ga.gov/MVP/mvp.do.

[9] King, Slide 5.

[10] Vote-by-mail ballots are often returned by voters at central drop-off points unconnected to the United States Postal Service. See discussion below addressing vote-by-mail directly.

[11] Digital return of ballots for counting is rare, and is primarily done in the case of some overseas ballots in a limited number of jurisdictions.

[12] North Dakota does not require voter registration. In some jurisdictions, registration may be automatic or available at the time of voting.

[13] Throughout this report, reference is made to statistics that include American states and the District of Columbia but not U.S. territories or commonwealths. This is due to the fact that some of the most authoritative data sources pertaining to election administration are inconsistent in the inclusion of data from territories/commonwealths.

The U.S. Election Assistance Commission's *Election Administration and Voting Survey* cited in this report, includes data provided by four territories—American Samoa, Guam, Puerto Rico, and the Virgin Islands—but does not include data from the Northern Mariana Islands.

[14] As mentioned in a previous footnote, North Dakota does not require voter registration. Rather, in North Dakota, voters need only provide photo identification and proof of age and residency at the time they vote.

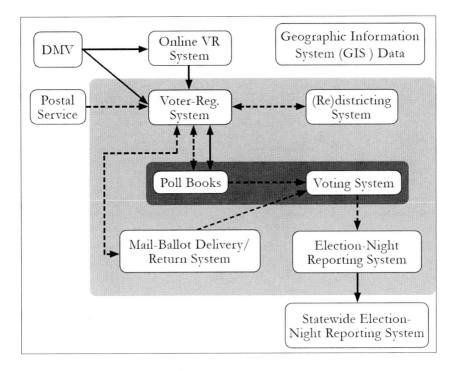

FIGURE 3-2 The interaction of election systems.
SOURCE: Stewart, Charles III, "The 2016 U.S. Election: Fears and Facts About Electoral Integrity," *Journal of Democracy,* April 2017, Vol. 28, No. 2, p. 56, Figure 2. © 2017 National Endowment for Democracy and Johns Hopkins University Press. Reprinted with permission of Johns Hopkins University Press.
NOTES: This schematic of voting information-system architecture is based on the work of Merle King. As a schematic, it does not include all conceivable election systems, e.g., systems used to pre-program ballot designs. For King's original figure, see http://www.nist.gov/sites/default/files/documents/itl/vote/tgdc-feb-2016-day2-merle-king.pdf (p. 14).
Arrows depict the direction of information flow between component systems. Solid lines indicate flows that typically rely on the Internet or other networks that are connected to the Internet; dashed lines indicate information flows that typically are "air-gapped" from outside networks. The dark box indicates systems that are typically deployed in individual polling places; the light-gray box indicates systems that are typically centralized in a local jurisdiction's election office.

cific geographic jurisdiction that is determined from the residential address that they provide for the purpose of voting. The voting address of record determines the voting district wherein a voter may cast a ballot. States set deadlines for when a voter must register to participate in an election.

Individuals may register to vote in many ways. They may register in person at election offices or at temporary sites set up in public places. They may register at departments of motor vehicles, departments of human services, and public assistance agencies.[15] All states offer the option to register to vote by mail. In 37 states and the District of Columbia, individuals can register to vote via the Internet so long as the registrant's information can be matched to information that was provided when a driver's license or other state-issued identification was issued.[16] Overseas voters and members of the U.S. armed forces and their dependents may obtain registration forms via electronic transmission.[17] Fifteen states currently allow same-day voter registration, and another, Hawaii, has enacted same-day registration provisions that take effect in 2018.[18] Nine states and the District of Columbia have introduced automatic voter registration (AVR).[19]

The 2002 Help America Vote Act (HAVA) established a requirement that all states implement a "single, uniform, official, centralized, interactive computerized statewide voter registration list." The list is to be administered by the state and contain the "name and registration information of every legally registered voter in the state."[20] To function as intended, each state voter registration database (VRD) must (1) add new registrants to the VRD; and (2) update information about voters (e.g., name and address changes).[21] These tasks require both good data and good matching procedures.

---

[15] The "Election Administration and Voting Survey: 2016 Comprehensive Report" (EAVS) states that, while state motor vehicle offices are the most common place where individual register to vote with 32.7 percent of all registrations, online registration has increased dramatically over the past 4 years (see p. i).

[16] See http://www.ncsl.org/research/elections-and-campaigns/electronic-or-online-voter-registration.aspx. Oklahoma has passed legislation to create online voter registration, but has yet to implement online voter registration.

[17] A subtitle of the National Defense Authorization Act for Fiscal Year 2010 (Pub.L. 111-84), the Military and Overseas Voter Empowerment Act ("MOVE" Act), required each state to designate not less than 1 means of electronic communication...for use by absent uniformed services voters and overseas voters who wish to register to vote or vote in any jurisdiction in the State to request voter registration applications." See Sec. 577.

[18] See http://www.ncsl.org/research/elections-and-campaigns/same-day-registration.aspx.

[19] "Automatic voter registration is an 'opt out' policy by which an eligible voter is placed on the voter rolls at the time they interact with a motor vehicle agency (or, in a few states, with other government agencies) unless they actively decline to be registered." See http://www.ncsl.org/research/elections-and-campaigns/automatic-voter-registration.aspx.

[20] HAVA § 303, 52 U.S.C. § 21083.

[21] Because voter registration lists are maintained by individual states, when a voter moves from one state to another, registration information does not follow the voter. As a consequence, the voter must register in his or her new state. Although voter registration forms ask new registrants whether they are registered in another state, the law does not require a voter to answer this question. As a result, it is common for individuals to appear on registration rolls in more than one state, even though they are only eligible to vote in one.

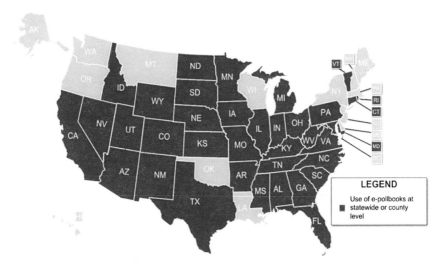

FIGURE 3-3 Electronic pollbook usage in the United States.
SOURCE: Adapted from Matthew Masterson, U.S. Election Assistance Commission, presentation to the committee, April 5, 2017, Washington, DC. The original image, which is available at: http://sites.nationalacademies.org/cs/groups/pgasite/documents/webpage/pga_178367.pdf, is the work of the U.S. Election Assistance Commission, taken or made during the course of an employee's official duties. As a work of the U.S. federal government, the image is in the public domain.

The VRD is used to prepare pollbooks. Pollbooks are used at polling places to verify an individual's eligibility to vote at the location where they have appeared. Traditionally, pollbooks were lists of registered voters that were printed and distributed to polling places in advance of an election, but increasingly, jurisdictions are using electronic pollbooks (EPBs or e-pollbooks). E-pollbooks are typically housed on laptops or tablets. Some contain local, static lists in electronic form, while others allow access to information in voter registration databases via a real-time Internet connection. According to the U.S. Election Assistance Commission, 36 states now use e-pollbooks (see Figure 3-3) in at least some of their jurisdictions.

BALLOTS

Across the country, jurisdictions use a variety of ballots (paper, card, or electronic) to present candidates and issues to voters. Ballots are often designed under multiple "constraints, including state laws on structure and ballot access rules, minority language requirements for jurisdictions covered by the VRA, the type of voting equipment used, and the various combinations of offices and issues for which people are eligible to vote."[22] Such constraints complicate the ballot design process.

A provisional ballot may be used to record the individual's vote if a voter's eligibility to vote cannot be established or if an election official asserts that the individual is not eligible to vote. Provisional ballots are required under HAVA, but states establish the criteria under which an individual may obtain a provisional ballot (see Appendix E).[23] Votes cast with provisional ballots are counted only after a voter's eligibility to vote has been established.

POLL WORKERS

On Election Day, paid temporary workers assist in polling place operations. These poll workers may verify the identity of a voter; assist voters in signing the register, affidavits, or other documents required to cast a ballot; provide a ballot to a voter; set up a voting machine; or carry-out other functions as dictated by state law.[24]

Many jurisdictions have difficulty recruiting and training poll workers because this "seasonal" work involves "long hours, low pay, workday conflicts that limit the recruiting pool, and increasing technological demands for special skills."[25] In 2016, "46.9 percent of responding jurisdictions reported having a somewhat difficult or very difficult time recruiting poll workers, compared with 22.7 percent that reported having a somewhat easy or very easy time. States and territories reported deploying an aver-

---

[22] Montjoy, Robert S., "The Public Administration of Elections," *Public Administration Review*, September-October 2008, pp. 792-793.

[23] See http://www.ncsl.org/research/elections-and-campaigns/provisional-ballots.aspx. Idaho, Minnesota, New Hampshire, North Dakota, Wisconsin, and Wyoming were exempt from the HAVA provisional ballot requirement as these are states that offered same day registration in 2002, the year HAVA was enacted. Nonetheless, some states that are not required to use provisional ballots have provisions for their use, and several states used provisional ballots before HAVA was enacted.

States where all ballots are returned by mail provide for the casting of provisional ballots. In Oregon, if a voter has a question about his or her eligibility to vote, he or she may request a provisional ballot from any Oregon County Elections Office (see http://sos.oregon.gov/elections/Documents/SEL113.pdf). In Washington, provisional ballots may be cast at any voter service center (see https://wei.sos.wa.gov/county/spokane/en/pages/FrequentlyAskedQuestions.aspx). Likewise, in Colorado, provisional ballots may be cast at voter service and polling centers (see https://www.sos.state.co.us/pubs/elections/FAQs/ElectionDay.html).

[24] "2016 Election Administration and Voting Survey" (EAVS), p. 13.

[25] U.S. Government Accountability Office, "Elections: Perspectives on Activities and Challenges Across the Nation" (Washington, DC: Government Printing Office, 2001), available at: https://www.gao.gov/new.items/d023.pdf.

In addition, poll workers must ensure compliance with numerous polling place mandates.

age of 7.8 poll workers per polling place for Election Day 2016."[26] Data provided on approximately 53 percent of poll workers who served in the 2016 federal election indicates that the poll worker population is skewed toward older individuals. Most poll workers are over age 40, 32 percent were between the ages of 61 and 70, and 24 percent were 71 years of age or older.[27]

While the qualifications required of poll workers vary by state, poll workers must often be registered to vote in the precinct or county in which they will serve. They must often also meet specific bilingual language requirements.

CASTING A VOTE

Voting Systems and the Voting Technology Marketplace

In the United States, voters cast votes using a variety of voting systems (see Figure 3-4). As discussed in Box 3-1, voting systems can be distinguished by the means of casting and tabulating votes. Voters have long cast their votes on paper (see Box 3-2), and paper remains the most commonly used medium in vote casting. The great majority of paper ballots are marked by the voter, and voter responses are tabulated using computerized optical scanners in a manner that is similar to systems used to record answers to standardized tests.[28] Alternatively, ballot-marking devices (BMDs) may be used in conjunction with optical scanners. In this scenario, a voter uses a touchscreen or keypad to select his or her choices on a digital display. When the voter has completed the selection process, a paper copy of the completed ballot is printed. This ballot can be scanned optically or digitally, but can also be read by humans. BMDs do not tabulate votes or record them in a computer's memory. Instead, the paper ballots are scanned and tabulated using a separate device.

Optical scan systems were the most commonly used voting system in U.S. counties in the 2016 election (see Table 3-1). In about one-third of U.S. counties, voters cast their ballots using BMDs or Direct Recording Electronic (DRE) systems where the voter casts his or her ballot using an electronic system (often similar to an ATM) (see Table 3-1). With DREs, ballots are then counted internally by the system's computer. In a small percentage of counties, voters either cast paper ballots that were manu-

---

[26] "2016 Election Administration and Voting Survey" (EAVS), p. 13.

[27] Ibid, p. 14.

[28] There are important differences. With standardized tests, for example, there are examination booklets with questions and separate sheets where students mark their selected answer by filling in ovals that correspond with their intended answer. With ballots, responses are marked by filling in ovals adjacent to the names of candidates or other choices.

Principal voting system, by county

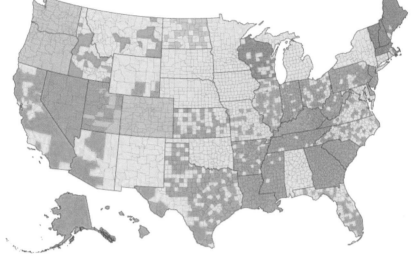

FIGURE 3-4 Voting systems across the United States.
SOURCE: Desilver, Drew, "On Election Day, Most Voters Use Electronic or Optical-Scan Ballots," Pew Research Center, November 8, 2016. Pew Research Center created the figure using data from the Verified Voting Foundation.

BOX 3-1
Overview of Vote Casting and Tabulation Methods

Systems in Use in Federal Elections

Hand-Marked "Optical" Scan Paper Ballot Systems. Voters mark paper ballots that are subsequently recorded electronically by scanning devices. On most scanned ballots, voters indicate their selections by filling in an oval or completing an arrow. Ballots may either be scanned on precinct-based optical scan systems in a polling place (precinct count) or collected in a ballot box to be scanned at a central location (central count). The original generation of optical ballot scanners used one row of optical sensors, one sensor per ballot column, to detect the voters' marks. Newer ballot scanners, sometimes referred to as "digital scanners," store an electronic image of each ballot [a "cast vote record" (CVR)], which can be used later if auditing of the election process is required.[a] The original generation

BOX 3-1 Continued

of ballot scanners used infrared sensors to detect ballot marks, giving rise to the generic term "optical scanner." Optical scanners are still used even though newer image-processing technologies are available.

Direct Recording Electronic (DRE) Systems. Voters use an electronic interface to record their votes directly into a computer's memory (e.g., onto a memory cartridge or memory card). That computer counts the vote. A keyboard is typically provided to allow entry of write-in votes, though older models have a paper roll behind a small opening where voters record write-in votes using a pen.

The first generation of DREs used a push-button interface, while later systems use a touchscreen interface or a dial interface.[b]

Some DREs are equipped with a voter-verifiable paper audit trail (VVPAT) feature that prints the voter's selections on paper and allows voters to confirm their selections by inspecting this paper before their votes are cast. The paper record is preserved and, depending on state election codes, may serve as the ballot of record in the event of an audit or recount.

Machine-Marked Paper Ballot Systems. A growing number of jurisdictions are using electronic "ballot-marking devices" (BMDs), which use electronic devices to mark paper ballots according to voters' instructions. The paper ballots are usually counted by optical scanners.

Hand Counted Paper Ballots. A small number of jurisdictions continue to manually count paper ballots cast in polling places.

Systems No Longer In Use In Federal Elections

Punch Card Voting Systems. Those systems employed a card (or cards) and a small clipboard-sized device for recording votes. Voters marked their choice by punching holes in the cards with a punch device. After voting, the voter either placed the ballot in a ballot box for later tabulation or the ballot was fed into a vote-tabulating device at the precinct. No jurisdictions used punch card voting systems in federal elections in 2016.

Mechanical Lever Voting Machines. First introduced in the 1890s, mechanical lever machines were used in many states during the 20th century. Voters would make choices by flipping levers and their selections were tabulated on machine counters similar to automobile odometers. As recently as 1996, mechanical lever machines were used by 20.7 percent of registered voters in the United States. Since 2010, no mechanical lever voting machines have been used in federal elections.

----

[a] Some scanners also store a digital photograph of the ballot.
[b] See Jones, Douglas W. and Barbara Simons, *Broken Ballots: Will Your Vote Count?* (Stanford: Center for Language and Information, 2012), pp. 91-101.

BOX 3-2
The Role of Paper in Elections

Until the widespread adoption of mechanical lever machines in the mid-20th century, hand-marked paper had been the most common medium upon which a voter cast a ballot. The cast paper ballot provided a physical record that could be examined in instances where a recount or other reconciliatory action was required. With the advent of mechanical lever machines, no record of a voter's choices was permanently stored, either on paper or mechanically—the only effect of casting a vote was to increment mechanical counters that accumulated the choices made by voters on a particular machine. Mechanical lever machines were popular where they were used. However, these machines were prone to breakdowns that could go undetected until balloting had ended.

Before the passage of the Help America Vote Act (HAVA), it was common for jurisdictions with lever machines to adopt electronic systems when they considered upgrading their voting systems. HAVA provided an impetus for jurisdictions that had previously used lever machines to adopt Direct Recording Electronic systems (DREs), either to provide accessible options for those with disabilities, or to replace paper-based systems altogether. The rapid growth in the prominence of DREs brought greater voice to concerns about their use, particularly their vulnerability to software malfunctions and external security risks. And as with the lever machines that preceded them, without a paper record, it is not possible to conduct a convincing audit of the results of an election.

Many electronic voting systems utilize paper as part of their operation. As discussed in Box 3-1, voters may mark paper ballots that are subsequently recorded electronically by scanning devices. Alternatively, ballot-marking devices may be used to mark paper ballots according to voters' instructions. In the case of DREs, there is no physical (i.e., paper) ballot. Instead, the ballot exists only in electronic form.

Problems arise when a voter does not actually verify his or her ballot, especially when the ballot is being tabulated by a computer that has a software flaw or is infected with malware (see Chapter 5). A ballot that is "voter marked" is by definition voter verified. Voters can verify that the selections on hand-marked ballots or on paper ballots produced by BMDs reflect their intended choices before their votes are tabulated. With DREs, voters may similarly verify their selections using a voter-verifiable paper audit trail (VVPAT) (see Box 3-1)—provided that the DRE is equipped with this feature. The information on a VVPAT may accurately present a voter's selections, but VVPATs exist independently of the record maintained in the DRE's computer memory. In most cases it is the electronic record, and not the VVPAT, that is used for vote tabulation.[a]

Paper Ballots Defined

Because records of ballots may take many forms, it is important to clearly define what is meant by "paper ballot." For the purposes of this report, references to paper ballots refer to original records that are produced by hand or a ballot-marking device, which are human-readable in a manner that is easily accessible for inspection and review by the voter without any computer intermediary (i.e., voter-verifiable), countable by machine (such as a scanner) or by hand, and which may be recounted or audited by manual examination of the human-readable portion of the ballot.

A paper ballot–based voting system makes the paper ballot the official "ballot of record" of the voter's expressed intentions. Other representations (e.g., an electronic representation produced by a scanner) are derivative and are not voter-verifiable. The human-readable portion of the cast paper ballot provides the basis for audits and recounts.

The Challenges of Paper Ballots

The use of hand-marked paper ballots can introduce voting errors. Voters may inadvertently make stray marks that can be misread by optical scanners. Voters using hand-marked paper ballots may accidentally skip a race or vote for multiple candidates in a race and thereby invalidate their vote for that particular race.[b] Counting paper ballots can be tedious, leading to vote-count errors.[c]

Paper ballots are not immune to fraud. Fraud may occur through ballot theft, destruction, or substitution, by ballot-box stuffing, or by the addition of marks to ballots after a voter finishes voting.[d]

Paper ballots can present logistical challenges when used in vote centers and in early voting, especially in densely populated, metropolitan areas. In vote centers and in early voting, every jurisdiction-specific ballot "style" that might conceivably be requested by a voter in a jurisdiction must be available at every voting site. In smaller jurisdictions, this functional requirement can be satisfied by having a physical inventory of every ballot style that might be requested at a site, through what is known as a "pick-and-pull" system. In larger jurisdictions that might have hundreds of ballot styles, maintaining a complete, secure inventory of ballot styles in every voting location may be logistically impossible or cost-prohibitive. One solution to this problem is a "ballot-on-demand" system, where appropriate ballots are printed on the spot for every voter. However, certain ballot-on-demand systems are costly and can put significant strain on the electrical systems of buildings hosting these systems.[e]

Electronic voting systems introduce challenges in and of themselves. Such systems are, for example, more costly than systems that use paper exclusively. Technical support for such systems is often necessary and adds to their cost over time. Such systems may also be more prone to breakdowns, are subject to technological obsolescence, and as is discussed in Chapter 5, vulnerable to cyberattacks and other threats. Furthermore, electronic systems must be stored in secure locations when not in use.

---

[a] As noted in Box 3-1, in some states, when a VVPAT is produced by a DRE, the VVPAT may be used as the ballot of record for election contests and recounts.

Research suggests that DRE VVPATs tend not to be voter verified. This suggests that VVPATs may be of little value as a check on the accuracy of DREs. See, e.g., Everett, S. P., "The Usability of Electronic Voting Machines and How Votes Can Be Changed Without Detection," doctoral dissertation, Rice University, Houston, Texas and Campbell, Bryan A. and Michael D. Byrne, "Now Do Voters Notice Review Screen Anomalies? A Look at Voting System Usability," *Proceedings of EVT/WOTE,* 2009.

continued

BOX 3-2 Continued

Research on the rate of voter verification of BMD ballots relative to the rate of verification of VVPATs or voter-marked paper ballots has been limited.

[b] Voters may also accidentally skip races when using DREs (see Chapter 4).

[c] For a discussion of the inherent weaknesses in human vote counting, see Goggin, Stephen N., Michael D. Byrne, and Juan E. Gilbert, "Post-election Auditing: Effects of Procedure and Ballot Type on Manual Counting Accuracy, Efficiency, and Auditor Satisfaction and Confidence," *Election Law Journal: Rules, Politics, and Policy*, 2012, Vol. 11, No. 1, pp. 36-51. A recount or audit can make use of limited software (e.g., spreadsheets) to assist in the counting.

Dr. Gilbert is a member of the committee that authored the current report.

[d] Such fraud provided motivation for the adoption of mechanical lever voting machines in the late 19th century.

[e] Power usage is determined by the type of printer required to produce the desired ballot. In instances where a printer must create an entire blank ballot certified to meet particular specifications using paper of a specific quality, be digitally readable, and be assigned a unique serial number, the necessary printer may draw significantly more power than is typical for printers used to print only voter selections on archival thermal paper.

TABLE 3-1 Types of Voting Systems Used in the United States in 2016

Voting System	Percent of U.S. Counties Using System
Hand Counted Paper Ballot	1.54%
Optical Scan	62.78%
Electronic (DRE or BMD)	32.85%
Mixed	2.69%

SOURCE: Brace, Kimball, President, Election Data Services, Inc., "The Election Process from a Data Perspective," presentation to the Presidential Advisory Commission on Election Integrity, September 12, 2017, Manchester, NH, available at: https://www.electiondataservices.com/wp-content/uploads/2017/09/BracePresentation2PenseCommAmended.pdf.

ally counted or voted with a mixture of systems (see Table 3-1). In many instances, marked ballots are submitted by mail and tabulated at a central location.

HAVA requires that each polling place used in a federal election

> be accessible for individuals with disabilities, including nonvisual accessibility for the blind and visually impaired, in a manner that provides the same opportunity for access and participation (including privacy and independence) [29] as for other voters . . . through the use of at least one

---

[29] Participation also includes the ability to cause one's own ballot selections to be recorded, verifying that one's ballot selections are correctly recorded, and the casting of one's self-verified ballot.

direct recording electronic voting system or other voting system equipped for individuals with disabilities at each polling place.[30]

Practically speaking, this means that even in local jurisdictions where ballots are typically cast by paper, DREs or other accessible voting systems are available in all polling places to comply with HAVA's accessibility requirements.

Further, HAVA requires that voting systems provide alternative language accessibility.[31] HAVA does not, however, provide a private right of action for voters with disabilities to pursue enforcement of either the disability or alternative language access provisions.[32] The 1990 Americans with Disabilities Act (ADA) may, however, provide a private right of action.[33]

Currently, there are only a few manufacturers of election systems. In the United States, three firms comprise 92 percent of the voting system market by voter reach.[34] The largest firm has about 460 employees.[35] This concentration represents a potential security risk, as a successful malicious infiltration of a single company could affect the operations of a significant portion of the election systems in use.

Certification of voting systems is an authority that rests with the states, although an important role in certification is played by the U.S. Election Assistance Commission (EAC) and the National Institute for Standards and Technology (NIST). Working collaboratively, the EAC and NIST maintain the Voluntary Voting System Guidelines (VVSG), which are a set of specifications against which voting systems are tested and which states may voluntarily adopt, in part or as a whole.[36] Several states require either testing to meet federal standards or testing by a federally accredited laboratory, and many states require full federal certification. In addition, many states have certification standards that meet or exceed federal standards (see Table 3-2).

---

[30] HAVA § 301(a)(3), 52 U.S.C. § 21081(a)(3).

[31] See HAVA § 301(a)(4), 52 U.S.C. § 21081(a)(4).

[32] See Golden, Diane Cordry, Association of Assistive Technology Act Programs, PowerPoint presentation to the committee (Slide 3), June 13, 2017, New York, NY. The presentation is available at: http://sites.nationalacademies.org/cs/groups/pgasite/documents/webpage/pga_180932.pdf. A private right of action is the right to bring a lawsuit.

[33] 42 U.S.C. §§ 12101 et seq.

[34] See University of Pennsylvania Wharton School, "The Business of Voting: Market Structure and Innovation in the Election Technology Industry," 2016, available at: https://publicpolicy.wharton.upenn.edu/live/files/270-the-business-of-voting. The three firms are Elections Systems & Software, Dominion Voting Systems, and Hart InterCivic.

[35] Ibid. That firm is Elections Systems and Software.

[36] The current version of the Voluntary Voting System Guidelines, VVSG1.1, was adopted by U.S. Election Assistance Commission commissioners on March 31, 2015. It is anticipated that the next iteration of the guidelines, VVSG 2.0, will be adopted in 2018. See https://www.eac.gov/voting-equipment/voluntary-voting-system-guidelines/.

TABLE 3-2 Voting Systems Certification Standards by State

States Requiring Testing to Federal Standards	States Requiring Testing by a Federally Accredited Laboratory	States Requiring Full Federal Certification (in Statute or Rule)
Connecticut, DC, Hawaii, Indiana, Kentucky, Nevada, New York, Tennessee, Texas, and Virginia	Alabama, Arkansas, Arizona, Colorado, Illinois, Iowa, Louisiana, Massachusetts, Maryland, Michigan, Minnesota, Missouri, New Mexico, Oregon, Pennsylvania, Rhode Island, Utah, and Wisconsin	Delaware, Georgia, Idaho, North Carolina, North Dakota, Ohio, South Carolina, South Dakota, Washington, West Virginia, and Wyoming

The following four states refer to federal agencies or standards, but do not fall into the categories above: Alaska,[a] California,[b] Kansas, and Mississippi. [c, d]

The following eight states have no federal testing or certification requirements. Statutes and/or regulations make no mention of any federal agency, certification program, laboratory, or standard; instead these states have state-specific processes to test and approve voting systems: Florida, Maine, Montana, Nebraska, New Hampshire, New Jersey, Oklahoma, and Vermont.

[a] In Alaska, the state elections director may consider whether the Federal Election Commission (FEC) has certified a voting machine when considering whether the system shall be approved for use in the state (though FEC certification is not a requirement).

[b] In California, the Secretary of State adopts testing standards that meet or exceed the federal voluntary standards set by the U.S. Election Assistance Commission.

[c] Mississippi requires that Direct Recording Electronic (DRE) systems shall comply with the error rate standards established by the FEC (though other standards are not mentioned).

[d] Even states that do not require federal certification typically still rely on the federal program to some extent and use voting systems created by vendors that have been federally certified.

SOURCE: Adapted from National Conference of State Legislatures, "Voting System Standards, Testing and Certification," available at: http://www.ncsl.org/research/elections-and-campaigns/voting-system-standards-testing-and-certification.aspx.

The software used to operate voting systems is generally proprietary; its purchase is bundled with the purchase of hardware and maintenance services.[37] The software installed on commercial election systems typically runs on a commercial off-the-shelf (COTS) operating system that is usually proprietary. There is a movement by some election administrators to

---

[37] Proprietary software is owned by a company or individual. The owner(s) of proprietary software typically place restrictions on how the software may be used. Users of proprietary software and other individuals outside of the company generally do not have access to the software's source code. As a result, they cannot modify the source code or view it to identify flaws or vulnerabilities.

Some states require the code to be escrowed and accessible for inspection in specified circumstances.

BOX 3-3
U.S. Government Accountability Office Survey on
Voting Equipment Use and Replacement

In a recent survey, the United States Government Accountability Office (GAO) "identified four key factors that jurisdictions and states consider when deciding whether to replace voting equipment[a]—(1) need for equipment to meet federal, state, and local voting system standards and requirements; (2) cost to acquire new equipment and availability of funding; (3) ability to maintain equipment and receive timely vendor support; and (4) overall performance and features of equipment."[b]

The survey also found that local election jurisdictions using "optical scan and direct recording electronic (DRE) . . . equipment during the 2016 general election . . . were generally satisfied with voting equipment performance." "Survey results indicated that accurate vote counting and efficiency of operation were top benefits experienced by jurisdictions for both types of equipment, and storage and transportation costs were a top challenge."[c]

In addition, stakeholders including state officials and voting equipment vendors "generally indicated that [. . . voluntary federal voting system] guidelines and their associated testing processes provide helpful guidance for equipment developers, cost savings for states that do not have to duplicate federal testing, and assurance that certified equipment meets certain requirements. However, some of these stakeholders stated that aspects of the guidelines could discourage the development of innovative equipment and limit the choices of voting equipment on the market." [d,e]

---

[a] The GAO report defines voting equipment as "the method or machine used to create ballots, cast and count votes, report election results, and maintain and produce audit trail information. It does not include other voting-related systems, such as those used for voter registration." See U.S. Government Accountability Office, "Observations on Voting Equipment Use and Replacement," April 11, 2018 (Washington, DC), p. 1, available at: https://www.gao.gov/products/GAO-18-294.

[b] Ibid, "Highlights of GAO-18-294."

[c] Ibid.

[d] Ibid.

[e] Ibid. For the survey, "GAO surveyed officials from a nationwide generalizable sample of 800 local jurisdictions (68 percent weighted response rate) and all 50 states and the District of Columbia (46 responded) to obtain information on voting equipment use and replacement. GAO also interviewed officials from (1) five jurisdictions, selected based on population size and type of voting equipment used, among other things, to illustrate equipment replacement approaches; and (2) seven voting system vendors, selected based on prevalence of jurisdictions' use of equipment, type of equipment manufactured, and systems certified, to obtain views on federal voting system guidelines."

develop or adopt open-source or publicly owned software that is available in source code form with a license, allowing the source code to be studied, modified, and distributed without limitation.[38] Open-source software is typically installed on commercial off-the-shelf equipment.

Election administrators take many factors into account when purchasing voting systems (see Box 3-3). Jurisdictions typically enter into software licensing and maintenance agreements with the vendors of commercial equipment. In exchange, the vendor maintains and provides hardware support for the election system and provides support for and upgrades to its proprietary software. In many jurisdictions, commercial vendors also provide the digital ballot definitions that enable their equipment to present, print, scan, and tabulate the jurisdiction's election-specific ballots for those casting votes.

Absentee Voting and Voting by Mail

Historically, voters were required to cast their ballots in person at their assigned polling places on Election Day. Absentee voting was originally developed to allow soldiers deployed away from home to vote. Eventually, the use of absentee ballots was extended to civilian voters, utilizing the mails to transmit and return ballots.[39]

Originally, voters had to provide an acceptable excuse to cast an absentee ballot, e.g., illness or travel. Today, however, most states have broadened voting mechanisms for the convenience of voters. Most states allow early in-person voting or voting by mail without requiring an excuse (see Figure 3-5).[40]

Three states, Washington, Oregon, and Colorado, have adopted mail-only voting. In these states, ballots are mailed to all registered voters. Voters may return completed ballots either by mail or in person. In 2016, most voters in these three states returned their ballots in person, rather than via

---

[38] Travis County in Texas, San Francisco, and Los Angeles County in California are three jurisdictions that are exploring the use of open-source operating systems. The state of New Hampshire recently adopted an open-source system called One4All based upon open-source software called Prime III developed at the University of Florida. Dr. Juan E. Gilbert, who serves as a member of the committee that authored the current report, was a developer of Prime III.

Software developers may also opt to make underlying source code available for others to review but not to modify without explicit permission. This scenario is sometimes referred to as disclosed source.

[39] Inbody, Donald S., *The Soldier Vote: War, Politics, and the Ballot in America* (New York: Palgrave Macmillan, 2016).

[40] Some states call all voting by mail early voting, whereas others refer to in-person early voting as a form of absentee voting. The use of different terms for what are essentially the same processes lends confusion to discussions of absentee or early voting.

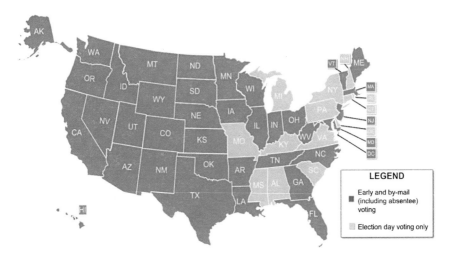

FIGURE 3-5 Early and by-mail (including absentee) voting in the United States.
SOURCE: Adapted from Masterson, Matthew, U.S. Election Assistance Commission, presentation to the committee, April 5, 2017, Washington, DC. The original image, which is available at: http://sites.nationalacademies.org/cs/groups/pgasite/documents/webpage/pga_178367.pdf, is the work of the U.S. Election Assistance Commission, taken or made during the course of an employee's official duties. As a work of the U.S. federal government, the image is in the public domain.
NOTE: For states designated as allowing "Election Day voting only," ballots received early may be cast if specific criteria are met.

the mail.[41] Thus, it is actually a misnomer to refer to these as "vote-by-mail" states. It is more accurate to refer to them as "ballot-delivery-by-mail" states.

Two other states, California and Utah, are moving toward mail-only elections. Currently, most voting in these states is conducted by mail.[42] In

---

[41] Stewart, Charles III, "2016 Survey of the Performance of American Elections: Final Report," 2017, p. 26. Dr. Stewart is a member of the committee that authored the current report.

[42] Masterson, Matthew, U.S. Election Assistance Commission, presentation to the committee, April 5, 2017, Washington, DC. See also "2016 Election Administration and Voting Survey" (EAVS), p. 9.

There are accommodations for in-person voting in the three states that conduct their elections by mail. In Washington, every county has a vote center for in-person voting (see https://www.sos.wa.gov/elections/faq_vote_by_mail.aspx). In Oregon, each County Elections Office provides privacy booths for voters who want to vote in person or voters who need assistance (see https://multco.us/file/31968/download). In Colorado, voters have the option to vote in person at a county Voter Service and Polling Center (VSPC) (see https://www.sos.state.co.us/pubs/elections/FAQs/ElectionDay.html).

2016, 52 percent of California's ballots and 68 percent of Utah's ballots were cast by mail.[43]

In addition, the Uniformed and Overseas Citizens Absentee Voting Act (UOCAVA) allows "U.S. citizens who are active members of the Uniformed Services, the Merchant Marine, and the commissioned corps of the Public Health Service and the National Oceanic and Atmospheric Administration, their eligible family members and U.S. citizens residing outside the United States" to vote using absentee ballots.[44]

Vote Centers

Traditionally, voters cast votes at assigned polling places within their specific precinct. Recently, in order to facilitate more efficient voting, numerous states have moved to consolidate voting in vote centers (see Figure 3-6). A vote center serves as a jurisdictional hub where any voter registered in that jurisdiction may vote, regardless of the precinct in which the voter resides.[45] Three states, Wyoming, South Dakota, and Iowa, allow jurisdictions to use vote centers only on Election Day. Twelve states and the District of Columbia allow jurisdictions to use vote centers during early voting only,[46] and eight states allow the use of vote centers during early voting and on Election Day.[47] California has authorized the use of vote centers starting in 2018.[48]

Collection Points for Ballots Received Early

Some jurisdictions provide secure facilities where voters may deposit ballots received early either before or on Election Day.

COUNTING VOTES

Votes are counted in three principal ways: (1) votes cast on paper ballots may be counted manually; (2) paper ballots may be scanned and the votes counted digitally; and (3) votes cast using electronic systems may be

---

[43] These percentages were calculated using the U.S. Census Bureau's, "Current Population Survey Voting and Registration Supplement," 2016. Utah did not report in the "2016 Election Administration and Voting Survey" (EAVS) the number of ballots cast by mail, which necessitated the use of a survey-based method to estimate vote-by-mail usage.

[44] 52 U.S.C. §§ 20301 *et seq.*

[45] See, for example, Colorado Revised Statutes 1-4-104 (49.8).Georgia, I

[46] The states are Florida, Georgia, llinois, Kansas, Louisiana, Maryland, Massachusetts, Nevada, North Carolina, Ohio, Tennessee, and West Virginia.

[47] The states are Arizona, Arkansas, Colorado, Indiana, New Mexico, North Dakota, Texas, and Utah.

[48] See http://www.ncsl.org/research/elections-and-campaigns/vote-centers.aspx.

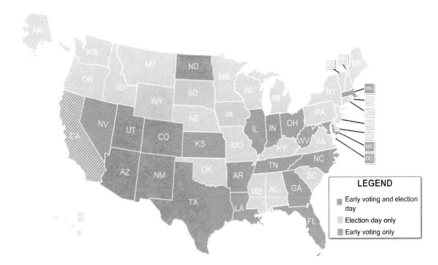

FIGURE 3-6 Vote centers in the United States.
The California Voter's Choice Act allows voters to cast ballots at vote centers in a limited number of counties beginning in 2018. See http://www.sos.ca.gov/elections/voters-choice-act/.
SOURCE: Masterson, Matthew, U.S. Election Assistance Commission, presentation to the committee, April 5, 2017, Washington, DC. The original image, which is available at: http://sites.nationalacademies.org/cs/groups/pgasite/documents/webpage/pga_178367.pdf, is the work of the U.S. Election Assistance Commission, taken or made during the course of an employee's official duties. As a work of the U.S. federal government, the image is in the public domain.

counted digitally. In the latter case, a paper ballot is not employed. When paper ballots are scanned, the results are tabulated, and printed, after the close of polls. The scanning may occur in one of two places—in the precinct where the ballots were cast, or in a central counting facility.

At the end of Election Day, if ballots were counted in the precinct, unofficial vote totals are communicated to a central election office through one of several means. These include paper printouts, hand-written paper forms, telephone, modem, and computer memory cards. Either on Election Day or soon thereafter, official returns are most likely to be communicated to the central office by traditional means, e.g., in paper form through the mails or via couriers.

Multiple safeguards are put in place to protect against tampering with vote counts.[49] These safeguards start at the point where the votes are

---

[49] In many states, safeguards were written into legislation prior to computerization and may not, therefore, offer the protections that they once did.

counted. States generally allow votes to be counted in the presence of the public, although these same laws may give precedence to some parts of the public (such as representatives of political parties) or require that the public be physically distanced from the vote counters. States commonly require that precinct vote returns be posted at the precinct once the counting is finished. This allows the public, candidates, and political parties an opportunity to record a precinct's vote count and subsequently compare it to totals published later.

States have laws that mandate the protection of ballots and other equipment used in elections, in the event a recount is necessary or if a count were to otherwise be called into question.

Ballots received by mail are typically sent directly to the central elections department. Mail-in ballots generally have two envelopes: an inner, plain envelope for the ballot; and an outer envelope with a signature line. The completed ballot is placed in the inner envelope, and the envelope is sealed. This envelope is then placed in the outer envelope, the outer envelope is sealed, and the voter signs on the signature line. When the ballot is received by the elections department, officials ensure that the signature on the outer envelope matches a signature on file with the department. If the signature matches, the inner envelope is removed and placed apart from the outer envelope. The inner envelopes are then opened and counted by an optical-scan reader or other mechanism.

CERTIFYING RESULTS

The tallies reported on election night are not the final results of the election. Instead, the official results of an election are not determined until the election returns have been validated through a process known as canvassing.[50] This validation involves not only rechecking the results reported on election night, but also adjudicating the status of provisional ballots and including ballots that may have arrived by mail after Election Day. Deadlines for the receipt of mail ballots vary by states, with many allowing mail ballots to be counted if they are postmarked before Election Day and arrive within a specified time after Election Day.[51] Once all vote numbers have been reconciled, the local election authority certifies the election for the jurisdiction and generates a report with the official vote count.[52] Results of statewide contests are further certified by state authorities, such as a state

[50] U.S. Election Assistance Commission, "Quickstart Management Guide: Canvassing and Certifying an Election," October 2008, p. 3, available at: https://www.eac.gov/assets/1/6/Quick%20Start-Canvassing%20and%20Certifying%20an%20Election.pdf.

[51] For a list of state deadlines from the 2016 election, see https://web.archive.org/web/20161108023142/https://www.vote.org/absentee-ballot-deadlines/.

[52] Ibid.

elections board. All states have laws that provide mechanisms to contest election results and to recount votes when election results are close.

ELECTION AUDITING

Most local jurisdictions conduct audits after an election, either because auditing is mandated by law or because local officials have independently adopted an audit requirement.[53,54] Some audits scrutinize the processes followed by election officials to ensure that proper procedures were followed. Such audits are referred to as performance audits.

Elections audits also may be conducted to reconcile the record of the number of voters who signed precinct pollbooks with the total number of ballots cast in the precinct and to check that the results of an election are consistent with the physical or electronic record that is produced by voters.

One recently developed class of post-election audits is risk-limiting audits.[55] Risk-limiting audits provide statistical assurance that a reported outcome is the same as the result that would be obtained if all ballots were examined by hand by ensuring that a different reported outcome has a high probability of being detected and corrected. Risk-limiting audits are typically performed by examining a random sample of the cast paper ballots and comparing their contents to expected results. Increasingly, election administrators are looking to risk-limiting audits to help ensure the accuracy and security of the vote and increase confidence in the outcome of elections. In 2018, Colorado will become the first state to conduct risk-limiting audits for a statewide election.[56]

---

[53] For a discussion of current state post-election audit practices, see, for example, National Conference of State Legislatures, "Post-Election Audits," available at: http://www.ncsl.org/research/elections-and-campaigns/post-election-audits635926066.aspx.

[54] Equipment used in elections may also undergo various forms of testing to attempt to improve integrity and security of election systems. These may include both pre-election and post-election testing of the hardware and software components of election systems. Pre-election testing of voting equipment is referred to as "logic and accuracy testing." Such pre-election testing is conducted primarily as an assurance against non-adversarial errors and breakdowns impacting accuracy.

[55] Philip B. Stark, Associate Dean, Division of Mathematical and Physical Sciences and Professor of Statistics, University of California, Berkeley, invented risk-limiting audits. Jennie Bretschneider, Office of the California Secretary of State; Sean Flaherty, Iowans for Voting Integrity; Susannah Goodman, Common Cause; Mark Halvorson, Citizens for Election Integrity Minnesota; Roger Johnston, Argonne National Laboratory; Mark Lindeman, Columbia University; Ronald L. Rivest, a member of the committee that authored the current report; and Pam Smith, Verified Voting, contributed to the development of Stark's work.

[56] Morrell, Jennifer, Arapahoe County (CO) Elections Director; Hilary Hall, Boulder County (CO) Clerk and Recorder; and Amber McReynolds, Denver (CO) County Elections Director, presentation to committee, December 7, 2017, Denver, CO.

CONCLUSION

For processes from voter registration to the casting and tabulation of votes, election administrators are responsible for the acquisition, maintenance, and oversight of numerous systems that often interact in complex ways. Each system plays an integral part in ensuring that the results of an election are consistent with the will of the voter. In Chapters 4, 5, 6, and 7, the committee provides its analyses of the challenges faced by the nation in achieving accurate elections and offers its recommendations to address these challenges.

4

Analysis of Components of Elections

In this chapter, the committee examines and provides recommendations regarding key components of U.S. elections. The topics discussed are voter registration and voter registration lists, absentee voting, pollbooks, ballot design, voting technology, and voting system certification. Weaknesses in any component can undermine the integrity of elections.

VOTER REGISTRATION AND VOTER REGISTRATION LISTS

Overview and Analysis

Federal and state laws and regulations govern voter eligibility. Federal law, for instance, stipulates that U.S. citizens of at least 18 years of age be entitled to vote in federal elections. State laws require that a voter be a resident (in some cases, resident for some minimum period of time, such as 30 days) of the state. Some states limit voter eligibility on the basis of criminal status or mental competency, although the specifics of such limitations vary. Some communities allow part-time residents who would otherwise be ineligible to vote to cast ballots in local election contests.

Constitutional provisions and federal statutes regulate how states administer voter registration. Since the 1960s, Congress has gradually expanded federal oversight of election administration and registration provisions. The Voting Rights Act (VRA) of 1965 prohibits discriminatory voting practices and prevents an individual from being denied the right to vote because of errors or omissions on registration materials that are not material to determining the voter's qualification to vote. Subsequent legislation aimed at facilitating voter registration includes the Voting Accessibility for the Elderly and Handicapped Act (VAEHA) of 1984 and the Uniformed and Overseas Citizen Absentee Voting Act (UOCAVA) of 1986. The National Voter Registration Act (NVRA) of 1993 requires that applications be made available at a variety of public locations and by mail and establishes broad guidelines concerning the maintenance of voter registration lists.[1]

The 2002 Help America Vote Act (HAVA) requires states to move from locally administered registration lists to state-level centralized, computerized voter registration lists. These state lists act as the official record of eligible voters for federal elections. HAVA requires regular maintenance of the lists for accuracy and completeness and stipulates that state or local officials should provide "adequate technological security measures to prevent the unauthorized access to the computerized" voter registration list.[2] The Act requires that a unique identifier be assigned to each legally registered voter in the state's voter registration list.[3] It states that applications for voter registration may not be accepted or processed by states without either a driver's license number, the last four digits of the applicant's Social Security number, or state-issued identification[4] and requires that those who register by mail present identifying information at the polls on Election Day the first time they vote (or with their mail-in ballots if voting by mail).[5]

An applicant's original signature on a voter registration form constitutes certification that the information provided is true, may be used to authenticate the identity of a voter if there are changes in the registrant's voting status, and often provides a means for authenticating the identity of the voter at a polling place or when processing absentee and/or mailed ballots.

If a voter registers to vote at a department of motor vehicles (DMV), relevant personal information may be provided at the DMV or extracted from the information in DMV files. This information is then transmitted electronically to the relevant election office with a copy of the signature

---

[1] Voting Accessibility for Elderly and Handicapped Act, 52 U.S.C. §§ 20101 et seq.; Uniformed and Overseas Citizens Absentee Voting Act, 52 U.S.C. §§ 20301 et seq.; National Voter Registration Act, 52 U.S.C. §§ 20501 et seq.

[2] HAVA, § 303.a.3, 52 U.S.C. § 21083. The Act does not specify what measures should be employed.

[3] HAVA, § 303.a.1.A, 52 U.S.C. § 21083.

[4] HAVA, § 303.a.5.A.i.I-II, 52 U.S.C. § 21083. "If an applicant for voter registration for an election for Federal office has not been issued a current and valid driver's license or a Social Security number, the State shall assign the applicant a number which will serve to identify the applicant for voter registration purposes. To the extent that the State has a computerized list in effect under this subsection and the list assigns unique identifying numbers to registrants, the number assigned under this clause shall be the unique identifying number assigned under the list (see Section 303.a.5.A.ii).

[5] HAVA, § 303.b.2.A.i.I-II, 52 U.S.C. § 21083.

on file with the DMV. When voters register entirely online, original signatures on file with DMVs or other agencies may be used for authentication purposes.

In those jurisdictions using the most common form of automatic voter registration, when an individual registers for a driver's license, information is shared with the state elections agency, where eligibility is established and, if eligible, the individual is registered to vote.[6] States have adopted various methods for individuals to opt out of registration, ranging from opting-out at the DMV to being notified of procedures to opt-out via a post card.[7]

Before adding individuals to a voter registration list, an attempt must be made to verify the information provided on a first-time voter registration application against the relevant state's department of motor vehicles database of driver's license numbers or the Social Security Administration's (SSA's) database of Social Security numbers. For a non-match, election administrators in most states will attempt to contact the applicant so that he or she can provide additional information. HAVA requires that an applicant who cannot be matched to a database be allowed to cast a provisional ballot on Election Day "upon the execution of a written affirmation by the individual . . . stating that the individual is . . . a registered voter in the jurisdiction in which the individual desires to vote; and" is "eligible to vote in that election."[8]

Federal law also requires states to establish a program "that makes a reasonable effort to remove the names of ineligible voters" from official voter registration lists.[9] States may use information supplied by the U.S. Postal Service (USPS) to identify registrants whose address may have changed.[10] To identify voters who have moved, election administrators often send periodic mailings to all voters in the jurisdiction or consult third-party move data. The envelope indicates that the mailing should not be forwarded and should be returned to the sender. Notices that are returned to the election official are an indication that the voter may have moved.

The databases containing voter registration lists often are connected, directly or indirectly, to the Internet or state computer networks. This connectivity raises concerns about unauthorized access to or manipulation of the registrant list or disruption of the registration system. Incidents of external intrusions have been reported recently:

---

[6] Some states have expanded the set of state agencies that can contribute new voters to the rolls, such as social service agencies and Alaska's Permanent Fund Dividend agency.

DMV databases are known to be unreliable.

[7] See National Conference of State Legislatures, "Automatic Voter Registration," available at: http://www.ncsl.org/research/elections-and-campaigns/automatic-voter-registration.aspx.

[8] See HAVA § 302.a, 52 U.S.C. § 21083.

[9] National Voter Registration Act of 1993 (NVRA) § 8.a.4, 52 U.S.C. §§ 20501–20511.

[10] NVRA, § 8.c.A, 52 U.S.C. §§ 20501–20511.

- In Illinois, Russian actors targeted and breached an online voter database in 2016 by exploiting a coding error.[11] For 3 weeks, they maintained undetected access to the system. Ultimately, personal information was obtained on more than 90,000 voters.[12]
- In California, hackers penetrated state registration databases and gained access to the personal information of a large number of voters.[13]
- In Georgia, more than 6.5 million voter records and other privileged information were exposed due to a server error. The security vulnerability had not been addressed 6 months after it was first reported to authorities, even though it could have been used to manipulate the state's election system.[14]

Election administrators usually rely on county or state government information technology (IT) departments to secure voter registration databases. In many cases, voter registration offices and election offices are separate departments in county government. In some cases, such as was the case in the Georgia example above, election data may be housed and managed in non-election offices.

Voter registration lists are used for many purposes other than establishing the eligibility of an individual to vote in an election. Voter registration lists are used, for example, by candidates and political parties to identify and contact potential voters.[15] At the local level, they are used to estimate how many people will vote, which helps guide election administrators as they prepare polling places for Election Day. These lists also are used in

---

[11] See Edwards, Brad, "Russian Hack into Illinois Election Database Was Worse Than Thought," CBS Chicago, June 13, 2017, available at: http://chicago.cbslocal.com/2017/06/13/russian-hack-into-illinois-election-database-was-worse-than-thought/; "Illinois Elections Board Offers More Information on Hacking Incident," WSIU, May 4, 2017, available at: http://news.wsiu.org/post/illinois-elections-board-offers-more-information-hacking-incident#stream/0; and Uchill, Joe, "Illinois Voting Records Hack Didn't Target Specific Records, Says IT Staff," The Hill, May 4, 2017, available at: http://thehill.com/policy/cybersecurity/331981-ill-voting-records-hack-didnt-target-specific-records-says-state-it.

[12] "Illinois Elections Board Offers More Information on Hacking Incident."

[13] See Reilly, Katie, "Russians Hacked Arizona Voter Registration Database—Official," Time, August 30, 2016, available at: http://time.com/4472169/russian-hackers-arizona-voter-registration/ and Uchill, Joe, "Hackers Demand Ransom for California Voter Database," The Hill, December 15, 2017, available at: http://thehill.com/policy/cybersecurity/365113-hackers-demand-ransom-for-california-voter-database.

[14] See Bajak, Frank, "APNewsBreak: Georgia Election Server Wiped After Suit Filed," Associated Press, October 27, 2017, available at: https://www.apnews.com/877ee1015f1c43f1965f63538b035d3f.

[15] See Hersh, Eitan, Hacking the Electorate: How Campaigns Perceive Voters (New York: Cambridge University Press, 2015).

some jurisdictions to establish signature and vote thresholds for petitions and referenda and to select jury pools.

Ideally, voter registration lists should include all eligible individuals who wish to be registered and no ineligible individuals. Voter registration lists should, therefore, be both accurate and complete. In this case, the term "accurate" can refer either to the factual correctness of the data that exist in the database or to the notion that the database contains none of the individuals not eligible to vote. The term "complete" refers to the presence in the database of all eligible individuals who wish to be registered.[16]

Maintenance of a voter registration list requires maintaining the currency of the registrant list and removing duplicate registrations and ineligible voters. This task requires comparing records within a voter registration list to other records to identify duplicate registrations (which are usually associated with changes of address or name) and comparing voter registration lists to other official lists that contain information about individuals who are ineligible to vote in a state, typically felons and individuals declared mentally incompetent.[17] Voter lists, of course, must be regularly compared against death registries. Data matching can draw either on intrastate sources, such as social service, motor vehicle, and death records or on interstate sources, such as the cross-state record matching performed by organizations such as the Electronic Registration Information Center (ERIC) and the Interstate Voter Registration Crosscheck System.[18,19,20] HAVA provides some criteria for developing and maintaining voter registration databases, and the U.S. Election Assistance Commission (EAC)

---

[16] See National Research Council, *Improving State Voter Registration Databases: Final Report*, (Washington, DC: The National Academies Press, 2010), available at: https://doi.org/10.17226/12788, p. 2.

[17] Ibid, p. 1.

[18] Data matching systems are imperfect. They can—and do—generate false matches that could potentially lead to the disenfranchisement of legitimate voters.

[19] ERIC "is a non-profit organization with the sole mission of assisting states to improve the accuracy of America's voter rolls and increase access to voter registration for all eligible citizens" (see http://www.ericstates.org/). As of the writing of this report, 22 states and the District of Columbia are members of ERIC. The 22 states are Alabama, Alaska, Arizona, Colorado, Connecticut, Delaware, Louisiana, Illinois, Maryland, Minnesota, Missouri, Nevada, New Mexico, Ohio, Oregon, Pennsylvania, Rhode Island, Utah, Virginia, Washington, West Virginia, and Wisconsin. See http://www.ericstates.org/faq.

[20] The Interstate Voter Registration Crosscheck System is operated by the office of the Secretary of State of the state of Kansas. The system compares voter rolls in participating states to identify potential duplicate voter registrations. It identifies voter registrations that have identical first names, last names, and dates of birth. According to the office of the Kansas Secretary of State, 28 states participated in Crosscheck in 2017. See http://www.wbur.org/radioboston/2017/11/03/massachusetts-crosscheck-system.

The system recently halted operations due to accuracy and security concerns raised by the U.S. Department of Homeland Security.

has issued guidance, but states maintain a degree of discretion in how to conform to these requirements.[21]

States have taken different approaches to building systems to meet the federal requirement for centralized voter registration lists. Under the so-called "top-down" approach followed by many states, state election administrators maintain a single, unified database and local election administrators provide the state with updates for the information needed in the database. Some states have instead opted for a bottom-up approach. In this scenario, local jurisdictions maintain their own registration lists but provide periodic updates to a separate statewide system. Other states use a hybrid approach that combines elements of both the top-down and bottom-up approaches.

The EAC's "2016 Statutory Overview" found that 38 states have voter registration databases that use a top-down approach, 9 have a hybrid system where counties manage their voter registration databases either through direct use of the state's database or independently using a third-party vendor (in the latter case, data is uploaded nightly to the state database), and 6 states employ a bottom-up approach.[22]

The USPS does not automatically notify election administrators of an individual's change of address. Election administrators must initiate address checks with USPS on their own. States may also obtain information on changes of address from departments of motor vehicles or other state agencies.

Two recent court decisions have significant implications for voter registration. In *Fish v. Kobach*, voters sued Kansas Secretary of State Kris Kobach for enforcing a state law that required Kansans to provide proof-of-citizenship documents in order to register to vote.[23] On June 18, 2018, the United States District Court for the District of Kansas found the law to be unconstitutional, because it created an unnecessary burden on voters. In *Husted v. A. Philip Randolph Institute*, the U.S. Supreme Court on June 11, 2018 upheld an Ohio law that allows the state to strike voters from the registration rolls if they fail to return a mailed address confirmation form and then do not vote for 4 years or two federal election cycles.[24] Lower courts had ruled that the law violated the National Voter Registration Act, which states that individuals may not be purged from the voter rolls because of a

[21] See HAVA, Section 303 and U.S. Election Assistance Commission, "Checklist for Securing Voter Registration Data," October 23, 2017, available at: https://www.eac.gov/documents/2017/10/23/checklist-for-securing-voter-registration-data/.

[22] See Green, Seth, "Statewide Voter Registration Systems," August 31, 2017, available at: https://www.eac.gov/statewide-voter-registration-systems/. A table that shows the approach employed by each state is available at this site.

[23] *Fish v. Kobach*, 2:16-cv-02105-JAR (D. Kan. 2018).

[24] *Husted v. A. Philip Randolph Institute*, 584 U.S. ___ (2018).

failure to vote. The Supreme Court concluded that the Ohio law does not deregister voters solely because of a failure to vote, but does so in conjunction with a failure to return an address confirmation form.

States have adopted numerous methods to facilitate voter registration: in person; by mail or fax; Internet; automatic registration; same-day registration. Each have advantages and disadvantages. Automatic voter registration may improve voter participation, reduce costs, and increase the accuracy of voter rolls. It may, however, needlessly register individuals who do not care to be registered, and if the systems are not well designed, it may be possible for noncitizens to end up on the voter rolls.[25] With regard to online registration, cost savings and voter convenience may be benefits. Security risks are, however, an inherent part of any online system.[26] For same-day registration, additional costs may be associated with system implementation (e.g., necessity to purchase additional equipment like e-pollbooks or ballot-on demand printers; costs of network connectivity; costs of updating voter registration systems to accommodate same-day registration, etc.). Some have suggested that same-day registration may increase voter turnout.[27]

Voter rolls inherently contain inaccuracies. Database maintenance is critical, but cannot yield perfect accuracy or completeness. It can be difficult to maintain the accuracy of voter registration lists due to changes in address, name, or life status. Sophisticated tools used in other industries may provide better record matching.[28] ERIC is one organization that attempts to make high-quality industry matching tools available to state election officials, but the existence of ERIC does not preclude states from exploring other record matching tools.

Electronic voter registration databases, like all electronic systems, are vulnerable to cyberattacks. If the contents of a voter registration database are altered or connectivity to a voter registration database is interrupted on Election Day either because of connectivity issues or because of efforts by external actors (e.g., by a denial-of-service attack), the consequences for voter convenience, voter confidence, and elections outcomes could be

---

[25] See http://www.ncsl.org/research/elections-and-campaigns/automatic-voter-registration.aspx.

[26] See http://www.ncsl.org/research/elections-and-campaigns/electronic-or-online-voter-registration.aspx.

[27] See http://www.ncsl.org/research/elections-and-campaigns/same-day-registration.aspx.

[28] For example: techniques for record linkage; the use of preprocessing to standardize data elements; accounting for the relative frequency of occurrence of values of strings such as first and last names; estimation of optimal matching parameters; and providing methods for estimating false match rates. See National Research Council, *Improving State Voter Registration Databases: Final Report* (Washington, DC: The National Academies Press, 2010), pp. 72-73, available at: https://doi.org/10.17226/12788.

very serious, especially if network-connected e-pollbooks are used and no backup of a voter registration list is available. Even if a voter registration database is not altered, the theft of the information contained in voter registration databases could cause serious problems. Driver's license numbers and Social Security numbers, for example, could be used for identity theft or for the purpose of requesting absentee ballots.[29] Attacks that alter voter registration data could be used to introduce fake or illegitimate voters, to remove valid voters from voter registration databases, or to force provisional voting on Election Day. The latter would likely be detected but could, nevertheless, cause long lines and other disruptions at polling sites. If an attacker targeted voters in jurisdictions that tend to favor one political party, such an attack could have a partisan effect on election results.

Even when a registration database is reasonably protected, online portals that allow voters to update their registration information can provide a point of entry for the alteration of data. Update requests often require weak authentication. In some states, the information required to change a registration is available from public records.

Findings

Simple voter registration methods encourage voter participation. Cumbersome voting registration systems may disenfranchise voters.

Voter registration databases face accuracy and completeness requirements that are in tension with one another. Measures to increase accuracy (e.g., purging suspect data) may reduce completeness. Measures to increase completeness (e.g., not purging suspect data) may reduce accuracy.

Electronic voter registration systems may make it easier to manage and maintain voter registration databases. The use of electronic information from other government sources may increase the accuracy and completeness of the databases.

Electronic voter databases are subject to cybersecurity vulnerabilities and attacks.

Election officials may not have the authority to request or insist on cybersecurity protections for voter registration databases or the resources to pay for appropriate cybersecurity measures.

Voter records contain personally identifiable information that, if compromised, could be used to the detriment of voters outside of the election context.

---

[29] Only a small number of states are permitted to collect Social Security numbers for voter registration purposes, although all states can collect the last four digits of Social Security numbers.

RECOMMENDATIONS

4.1 Election administrators should routinely assess the integrity of voter registration databases and the integrity of voter registration databases connected to other applications. They should develop plans that detail security procedures for assessing voter registration database integrity and put in place systems that detect efforts to probe, tamper with, or interfere with voter registration systems. States should require election administrators to report any detected compromises or vulnerabilities in voter registration systems to the U.S. Department of Homeland Security, the U.S. Election Assistance Commission, and state officials.

4.2 Vendors should be required to report to their customers, the U.S. Department of Homeland Security, the U.S. Election Assistance Commission, and state officials any detected efforts to probe, tamper with, or interfere with voter registration systems.

4.3 All states should participate in a system of cross-state matching of voter registrations, such as the Electronic Registration Information Center (ERIC). States must ensure that, in the utilization of cross-matching voter databases, eligible voters are not removed from voter rolls.

4.4 Organizations engaged in managing and cross-matching voter information should continue to improve security and privacy practices. These organizations should be subject to external audits to ensure compliance with best security practices.

VOTING BY MAIL, INCLUDING ABSENTEE VOTING

Overview and Analysis

Absentee voting (voting remotely) provides an opportunity to cast a vote by obtaining a ballot (usually a printed ballot obtained by mail) in advance of an election and returning the completed ballot to elections officials by mail[30] or other means. If paper ballots are used, voters typically mark the received ballot and place it in a secrecy envelope or sleeve. The envelope/sleeve is then placed into a second mailing envelope. The voter seals the mailing envelope and signs an affidavit on the envelope's exterior. The ballot is then mailed to the appropriate elections office or deposited at a designated dropoff location.[31] To be counted, absentee ballots must be postmarked, deposited, or received by a deadline that is generally estab-

---

[30] In at least 22 states, certain elections may be conducted entirely by mail. See http://www.ncsl.org/research/elections-and-campaigns/all-mail-elections.aspx.

[31] See http://www.ncsl.org/research/elections-and-campaigns/all-mail-elections.aspx.

lished by state governments. In many jurisdictions, the identity of the voter is confirmed by matching the signature on the envelope against the signature in the voter registration database.[32]

As discussed in Chapter 3, three states, Washington, Oregon, and Colorado principally use the mails to distribute ballots to all registered voters, and two others, California and Utah, are moving toward this model.[33] In these instances, ballots are mailed to all registered voters. Other "states permit all-mail elections in certain circumstances, such as special districts, municipal elections, when candidates are unopposed, or at the discretion of the county clerk."[34]

In some jurisdictions, signature matching is completed automatically by a computer that compares the signature on a scanned paper ballot to signatures on file in a database. In other jurisdictions, a non-expert election administrator compares signatures. Both methods can result in mismatching. In addition, an individual's signature may change over time. If a signature database is not updated regularly, mismatching may occur. Inaccurate matching may result in the rejection of valid ballots.

Ninety-nine percent of absentee ballots categorized as "returned and submitted for counting" were ultimately counted in the 2016 federal election.[35] In 2016, the most common reasons that absentee ballots were rejected were that the signature on the ballot did not match the signature in a state's records, that the required signature was missing, or that the ballot was received after deadline.[36]

UOCAVA allows "U.S. citizens who are active members of the Uniformed Services, the Merchant Marine, and the commissioned corps of the Public Health Service and the National Oceanic and Atmospheric Administration, their eligible family members and U.S. citizens residing outside

---

[32] Some states accommodate remote accessible ballot marking. In such states, a voter retrieves and marks a ballot online, prints out the completed ballot, and mails the ballot to the appropriate elections office. See, e.g., https://nfb.org/ohio-requires-accessible-absentee-ballots-blind; https://www.sos.state.oh.us/globalassets/elections/directives/2018/dir2018-03.pdf; https://leginfo.legislature.ca.gov/faces/billNavClient.xhtml?bill_id=201520160AB2252; and http://sfgov.org/elections/remote-accessible-vote-mail-system.

[33] Masterson, Matthew, U.S. Election Assistance Commission, presentation to the committee, April 5, 2017, Washington, DC. See also "2016 Election Administration and Voting Survey" (EAVS), p. 9.

In Washington, every county has at least one vote center for in-person voting (see https://www.sos.wa.gov/elections/faq_vote_by_mail.aspx). In Oregon, each county elections office provides privacy booths for voters who want to vote in person or voters who need assistance (see https://multco.us/file/31968/download). In Colorado, voters have the option to vote in person at a county Voter Service and Polling Center (VSPC) (see https://www.sos.state.co.us/pubs/elections/FAQs/ElectionDay.html).

[34] See http://www.ncsl.org/research/elections-and-campaigns/all-mail-elections.aspx.

[35] "2016 Election Administration and Voting Survey" (EAVS), p. 10.

[36] Ibid.

the United States" to vote using absentee ballots.[37] UOCAVA voters must have a legal voting residence in the jurisdiction where they want to vote.[38] The USPS and the Military Postal Service Agency (MPSA) have special procedures for handling UOCAVA outgoing and incoming ballots.[39]

In 2009, Congress amended portions of UOCAVA with the Military and Oversees Voter Empowerment Act (MOVE). MOVE stipulates that ballots requested by UOCAVA voters must be transmitted 45 days before a federal election, that voters have the right to receive their ballots by at least one electronic method (email, online, or fax) *or* by mail, and that states must have a system in place to determine whether a ballot was received by the appropriate elections office.[40]

To be counted, UOCAVA ballots must be returned to the appropriate election office before a state-mandated deadline.[41] In 2016, states reported transmitting 930,156 UOCAVA ballots. Of this number, 633,592 were returned.[42] Approximately 110,000 more ballots were transmitted to overseas citizens than to uniformed services voters.[43] Of the UOCAVA ballots returned by voters, 512,696 (80.9 percent) were counted.[44]

Absentee voting introduces benefits and risks that are different from the benefits and risks of in-person voting.[45] By-mail voting increases convenience, especially for the disabled community, and may improve the amount of thought that goes into marking a ballot. A common justification for voting by mail is increasing the amount of deliberation voters give to their ballots. However, the evidence presented to support this claim tends to be anecdotal or based on appeals to logic. There appears to be no peer-reviewed empirical research to quantify the degree to which increased voter knowledge or deliberation is associated with expanding mail-ballot opportunities. There is evidence, though, that the convenience of by-mail voting

---

[37] See https://www.fvap.gov/info/laws/uocava.

[38] See U.S. Election Assistance Commission, "Tips for Helping UOCAVA Voters and their Families," p. 3, available at: https://www.eac.gov/documents/2017/08/03/six-tips-for-helping-uocava-voters-and-their-families-from-eac-contingency-plan-election-administration-pre-election-security/.

[39] Ibid, p. 6.

[40] Ibid, p. 2.

[41] Ibid, p. 12.

[42] Ibid.

[43] Ibid, p. 11.

[44] Ibid, p. 12.

[45] Stewart, Charles III, "Losing Votes by Mail," *New York University Journal of Legislation and Public Policy 13*, 2010, No. 3, pp. 573-601. Dr. Stewart is a member of the committee that authored the current report.

may stimulate increased voter turnout in certain situations.[46] There are other indications, however, that by-mail voting may initially increase voter turnout rates but that rates then revert to previous turnout patterns and that by-mail voting can depress turnout in presidential and gubernatorial general elections.[47] Further, all-mail voting may produce a cost savings.[48] For instance, in a study of Colorado's 2013 mandate that mail ballots be sent to all registered voters, the Pew Charitable Trusts estimated that this reform decreased costs by an average of 40 percent, in addition to reducing the use of provisional ballots by 98 percent.[49]

Remote voting creates new opportunities for coercion and for loss of privacy that in-person voting attempts to overcome.[50] Outside of the privacy of a voting booth, other individuals may buy or sell votes or overtly pressure a voter to make particular ballot selections. Ballots may be stolen or intercepted by third parties who mark and cast them. It may also be easier for an election administrator to examine a ballot before it is separated from its identifying outer envelope or email header. In the case of all-mail voting, the dependence on written instructions rather than poll-worker assistance may disadvantage some voters and increase the residual vote rate.[51]

The paths that mail ballots travel introduce other risks that are typically avoided with in-person voting. Most absentee and mail balloting relies on the U.S. postal system to (1) deliver the request for an absentee ballot from the voter to the local jurisdiction; (2) deliver the unmarked ballot from

---

[46] See Gerber, Alan S., Gregory A. Huber, and Seth J. Hill, "Identifying the Effect of All-mail Elections on Turnout: Staggered Reform in the Evergreen State," *Political Science Research and Methods*, 2013, Vol. 1, No. 1, pp. 91-116; Miller, Peter and Sierra Powell, "Overcoming Voting Obstacles: The Use of Convenience Voting by Voters with Disabilities," *American Politics Research*, 2016, Vol 44, No. 1, pp. 28-55; and Flaxman, Seth, Marie-Fatima Hyacinthe, Parker Lawson, and Kathryn Peters," Voting by Mail: Increasing the Use and Reliability of Mail-Based Voting Options," available at: http://web.mit.edu/supportthevoter/www/files/2013/11/Vote-by-Mail-Reform-Memo.pdf.

[47] See, e.g., https://www.eac.gov/documents/2017/02/23/will-vote-by-mail-elections-increase-turnout/.

[48] See "Voting by Mail: Increasing the Use and Reliability of Mail-Based Voting Options."

[49] Pew Charitable Trusts, "Colorado Voting Reforms: Early Results," available at: http://www.pewtrusts.org/-/media/assets/2016/03/coloradovotingreformsearlyresults.pdf.

[50] See http://www.ncsl.org/research/elections-and-campaigns/all-mail-elections.aspx.

[51] Alvarez, R. Michael, Dustin Beckett, and Charles Stewart III, "Voting Technology, Vote-by-Mail, and Residual Votes in California, 1990–2010," *Political Research Quarterly*, 2013, Vol. 66, No. 3, pp. 658-670.
"Residual votes" are the sum of over- and under-votes on a ballot, typically measured at the top of the ticket. See Stewart, Charles III, "Voting Technologies," *Annual Review of Political Science*, 2011, Vol. 14, pp. 353-378. Dr. Stewart is a member of the committee that authored the current report.

the jurisdiction back to the voter; and (3) deliver the marked ballot back to the election jurisdiction for counting.

The marked ballot is a more valuable target than a request for a mail ballot or even the unmarked ballot. The secrecy associated with marked ballots makes it more difficult for a voter to detect whether a marked ballot has been tampered with or intercepted.

The heavy reliance on the U.S. postal system for mail ballots introduces potential problems related to inconsistencies in service. "Mail delivery is not uniform across the nation. Native Americans on reservations may in particular have difficulty. Many do not have street addresses, and their P.O. boxes may be shared."[52] The mail return of marked ballots may be delayed past the deadline. Since, currently, there are no agreed upon chain-of-custody procedures for mailed ballots, mail-in voting presents more chances for votes to be lost than is the case with in-person voting. Collection points for mail-in ballots reduce dependence on the postal system and provide voters with greater assurance that their ballots will be received.[53]

Because of concerns about the chain-of-custody of mail ballots, local election officials—often in direct cooperation with the USPS—have adopted practices to allow officials and voters to track the location of mail ballots through the mail stream.[54] These systems allow postal mail to be tracked via the USPS's Intelligent Mail Barcode. There are services available to election officials to facilitate the use of this data, including products like Ballot Scout, Ballot Tracks, and Ballot Trace.[55]

Concerns over the speed and reliability of the USPS have led to the replacement of the mails with electronic means, particularly the Internet, in the administration of voting by mail in many jurisdictions. While there are administrative gains to be had by moving to the electronic transmission of absentee ballot requests, and the transmission of unmarked ballots to voters, this practice comes with many of the cybersecurity vulnerabilities discussed in Chapter 5 of this report. However, because there are also vulnerabilities with using the mails to request absentee ballots and transmit unmarked ballots to voters, it may be that relying on the Internet for these portions of the vote-by-mail system could lead to a net improvement

---

[52] See http://www.ncsl.org/research/elections-and-campaigns/all-mail-elections.aspx.

[53] Stewart, Charles III, "Losing Votes by Mail," *Journal of Legislation and Public Policy*, Vol. 13, No. 3, pp. 573-601. Dr. Stewart is a member of the committee that authored the current report.

[54] Bipartisan Policy Center, "The New Realities of Voting by Mail in 2016," June 2016, available at: https://bipartisanpolicy.org/wp-content/uploads/2016/06/BPC-Voting-By-Mail.pdf.

[55] In the 2014 federal election, 35 states had tools on their state election websites that allowed voters to track their absentee ballots. See Pew Charitable Trusts, "Elections Performance Index," available at: http://www.pewtrusts.org/en/multimedia/data-visualizations/2014/elections-performance-index#indicatorProfile-OLT.

in the administration of mail-balloting. However, it appears that no peer-reviewed research has comprehensively assessed the relative risk-reward tradeoffs involved in using the mails to transmit absentee ballot requests and unmarked ballots.

Few marked ballots are currently transmitted electronically. The electronic transmission of absentee ballots—via fax, email, or web portal—is most often reserved for voters who fall under UOCAVA "as these voters often face unique challenges in obtaining and returning absentee ballots within state deadlines."[56] Three states, Arizona, Missouri, and North Dakota, allow some voters to return marked ballots using a web-based portal, but Missouri only offers electronic ballot return for military voters serving in a "hostile zone."[57] In North Dakota and Arizona, any UOCAVA voter may use the web option.[58] The singular importance of the marked ballot may help explain why few marked ballots are currently transmitted electronically.

Findings

Vote-by-mail may increase convenience and satisfaction, as voters may complete ballots from the comfort of their home and devote as much time as they wish to assess candidates and issues.

Vote-by-mail can make voting more accessible for individuals with disabilities.

---

[56] See http://www.ncsl.org/research/elections-and-campaigns/Internet-voting.aspx.

[57] "Alabama conducted a pilot project in 2016 to permit UOCAVA voters located outside of U.S. territorial limits to submit voted ballots via a web portal, but the state has not made this program permanent. Alaska previously made a web portal available to any absentee voter to return a voted ballot, but discontinued this option in 2018." See http://www.ncsl.org/research/elections-and-campaigns/Internet-voting.aspx.

The state of Washington allows all voters to return ballots as email attachments—although non-UOCAVA voters must follow up with a physical ballot to have their electronic ballots counted.

The West Virginia Secretary of State has recently announced a pilot to offer voting via mobile devices to military voters. See https://sos.wv.gov/News-Center/Pages/Military-Mobile-Voting-Pilot-Project.aspx.

[58] See http://www.ncsl.org/research/elections-and-campaigns/Internet-voting.aspx.

Twenty-one states (Colorado, Delaware, Hawaii, Idaho, Indiana, Iowa, Kansas, Maine, Massachusetts, Mississippi, Montana, Nebraska, Nevada, New Jersey, New Mexico, North Carolina, Oregon, South Carolina, Utah, Washington, and West Virginia) and the District of Columbia allow some voters to return ballots via email or fax.

Seven states (Alaska, California, Florida, Louisiana, Oklahoma, Rhode Island, and Texas) allow some voters to return ballots via fax.

Nineteen states (Alabama, Arkansas, Connecticut, Georgia, Illinois, Kentucky, Maryland, Michigan, Minnesota, New Hampshire, New York, Ohio, Pennsylvania, South Dakota, Tennessee, Vermont, Virginia, Wisconsin, and Wyoming) do not allow electronic return of ballots. Voters must return voted ballots via postal mail. See http://www.ncsl.org/research/elections-and-campaigns/Internet-voting.aspx.

Vote-by-mail may produce cost savings.

Vote-by mail requires careful design of ballot transmittal envelopes and tabulation procedures.

With vote-by-mail, it is not possible to guarantee that a voter has cast his or her ballot privately. A voter might be coerced into making particular selections.

Currently, there are no agreed upon chain-of-custody procedures for mailed ballots. Vote-by-mail presents more chances for votes to be lost than is the case with in-person voting.

Drop boxes for mail-in ballots outside of elections offices reduce dependence on the postal system.

Collection points for mail-in ballots introduce additional points of failure and security concerns.

Election jurisdictions are increasingly adopting programs that allow officials and voters to track the location of mail ballots.

All-mail elections may slow down the vote counting process, especially if ballots are accepted according to postmark date (and thus may be received and counted days or weeks after the election).

UOCAVA voting presents unique challenges for election administration with regard to the transmission of ballots to and from remote locations.

RECOMMENDATION

4.5   All voting jurisdictions should provide means for a voter to easily check whether a ballot sent by mail has been dispatched to him or her and, subsequently, whether his or her marked ballot has been received and accepted by the appropriate elections officials.

POLLBOOKS

Overview and Analysis

When a voter arrives at a polling place, the voter typically "checks in" to vote by providing a name and/or some form of identification to a poll worker, who matches the given name to information in a pollbook.[59] In some states, voters may be required to fulfill a non-documentary identification requirement. In lieu of presenting a document that establishes their identity, they might, for instance, be required to sign an affidavit asserting eligibility to vote, provide a signature, or provide personal information either orally or in writing. Once an individual's eligibility to vote has been

---

[59] Thirty-four states have laws requesting or requiring voters to show some sort of identification at the polls. See http://www.ncsl.org/research/elections-and-campaigns/voter-id.aspx.

determined, an eligible voter may proceed to cast a vote. If an individual's eligibility cannot be confirmed, that individual must be offered the opportunity to cast a provisional ballot. The procedures for when to issue and count provisional ballots are established by individual states.[60]

While most jurisdictions (81.8 percent) still use preprinted paper registration lists to check in voters, between the 2012 to 2016 federal elections, there was a 75 percent increase in the use of electronic pollbooks (e-pollbooks) where paper is replaced by computers either containing locally stored lists of registered voters or connected to digital voter registration databases via the Internet. In the 2016 election, at least 1,146 jurisdictions (17.7 percent of all jurisdictions) used e-pollbooks.[61] Because larger jurisdictions tend to use e-pollbooks, the fraction of voters checked-in using e-pollbooks is close to 50 percent.[62]

E-pollbooks provide more data to poll workers than traditional paper pollbooks. E-pollbooks may be networked and receive immediate updates on who has voted in other voting locations. They may allow poll workers to look up voters from an entire county or state or notify a poll worker that a voter has already voted.[63] A poll worker may use an e-pollbook to direct a voter to the correct polling location. E-pollbooks may also host on-demand training tips and procedural guides for poll workers. "Some e-pollbooks can scan driver's licenses, speeding up the voter check-in process. Other e-pollbooks use an electronic signature pad that immediately captures the voter's signature."[64] E-pollbooks may also produce turnout numbers and lists of those who voted.[65]

The requirements for the certification of e-pollbooks vary considerably among the states and jurisdictions that permit their use.[66] As of March 2017, only eight states certify e-pollbooks. Eleven states have statutes

---

[60] See Appendix E.

[61] "2016 Election Administration and Voting Survey" (EAVS), p. 8.

[62] This figure was calculated directly from the Election Administration and Voting Survey dataset available on the website of the U.S. Election Assistance Commission at https://www.eac.gov/research-and-data/election-administration-voting-survey/.

[63] With regard to absentee ballots, standard practice is to check voter registration systems to see whether the voter is recorded as having already voted. If an individual has returned an absentee ballot prior to Election Day, this information should be reflected in the poll book (whether it is electronic or not). If the absentee ballot arrives after Election Day and the voter cast a ballot on Election Day, the absentee ballot should be reflected in the voter registration system. The issue of multiple voting is most critical in jurisdictions with multiple vote centers. In this instance, it is important that e-pollbooks be updated in real time.

[64] See Hubler, Katie Owens, "All About E-Poll Books," *NCSL's The Canvass*, Issue 46, February 2014, available at: http://www.ncsl.org/research/elections-and-campaigns/the-canvass-february-2014.aspx#Poll%20Books.

[65] Ibid.

[66] In general, to achieve certification, a system must undergo independent testing to verify that it meets specified requirements for design and performance.

explicitly authorizing the use of e-pollbooks, three states have statutes referring to e-pollbooks without explicitly authorizing their use, five states have established procedures or certification requirements dictated by the state but not by statute, and three states have jurisdictions that used e-pollbooks absent mention in statute or rule.[67]

While attacks on e-pollbooks could be used to change voter data, prevent access to voter registration data, fool the devices' check-in logic to allow multiple voting by individuals, or access back-end systems, there are no national security standards for e-pollbooks.[68] As a result, security practices vary across states. Some states conduct testing before each election, some make backup e-pollbooks available on Election Day, and some make backup paper rolls available on Election Day. Others leave testing or audits up to individual counties or provide no backup system.[69]

The static nature of printed pollbooks presents several problems, because voter registration recruitment continues until the registration deadline.[70] Voter registration offices may not be able to finish entering registrant data into voter registration databases before pollbooks must be printed for distribution to polling places. In light of this, some voter registration offices create supplemental lists for distribution to election judges immediately prior to an election. The success of this approach depends on numerous logistical factors (e.g., timely delivery).

Paper pollbooks may present a risk in the context of convenience programs like vote centers and early voting, as the use of paper pollbooks would not prevent a voter from casting a ballot in more than one location. In such scenarios, multiple voting may only become apparent after the fact, and documentation may not be enough for successful prosecution. While voter registration offices may be contacted to qualify each voter, voter registration call centers have limited capacity, and cell phone service at polling places may not be reliable.

Provided that they are properly counted, the use of provisional ballots offers a potential solution to a compromised e-pollbook system. However, if an e-pollbook system were compromised to the point that a jurisdiction had to rely solely on provisional ballots, it is likely that the delays produced by the provisional ballot procedure, and the attending chaos at

[67] See http://www.ncsl.org/research/elections-and-campaigns/electronic-pollbooks.aspx.

[68] See Norden, Lawrence and Ian Vandewalker, Brennan Center for Justice, "Securing Elections from Foreign Interference," 2017, available at: https://www.brennancenter.org/sites/default/files/publications/Securing_Elections_From_Foreign_Interference_1.pdf.

[69] See Pew Charitable Trust, "A Look at How—and How Many—States Adopt Electronic Poll Books," available at: http://www.pewtrusts.org/en/multimedia/data-visualizations/2017/a-look-at-how-and-how-many-states-adopt-electronic-poll-books.

[70] The move in many jurisdictions to same-day registration means that the contents of pollbooks may be in flux even on Election Day.

the polls, would produce significant problems with voter confidence—and perhaps disenfranchise voters. Nonetheless, if paper poll books are used in emergencies, it will be possible to determine the number of illegal multiple votes after the election ends. This acts not only as a deterrent to unlawful voting but as a mechanism for determining whether illegal votes may have changed the outcome of an election.

The move in many jurisdictions to same-day registration and early voting makes it necessary to provide distributed access to pollbooks and real-time information on those who are registered to vote or who have voted. This reliance on connectivity presents cybersecurity risks.

E-pollbooks help to ensure that an individual casts only a single ballot as they are able to offer, through online connectivity, access to the most current version of the voter registration database. Voter registration offices can focus on data entry through the early voting period—and even up to Election Day—since data entry need not be completed to meet the cut-off time for the printing and delivery of paper pollbooks.

Findings

Eligible voters may be denied the opportunity to vote a regular ballot if pollbooks are inaccurate.

Internet access to e-pollbooks increases the risks associated with the use of e-pollbooks to manage elections. Cyberattacks can alter the voter registration databases used to generate and update pollbooks. If pollbooks are altered by external actors, eligible citizens might, on election days, be denied the right to vote or ineligible individuals might be permitted to vote. Cyberattacks could also compromise the record of who actually voted on Election Day—or disrupt an election in numerous other ways.

If an e-pollbook is connected to a remote voter registration database and there is no offline backup, a denial-of-service cyberattack could force voting to be halted.

Cybersecurity risks are a factor for consideration when making the decision to use Internet-connected e-pollbooks.

RECOMMENDATIONS

4.6 Jurisdictions that use electronic pollbooks should have backup plans in place to provide access to current voter registration lists in the event of any disruption.

4.7 Congress should authorize and fund the National Institute of Standards and Technology, in consultation with the U.S. Election Assistance Commission, to develop security standards and verification and validation protocols for electronic pollbooks in addition to the standards and verification and validation protocols they have developed for voting systems.

4.8 Election administrators should routinely assess the security of electronic pollbooks against a range of threats such as threats to the integrity, confidentiality, or availability of pollbooks. They should develop plans that detail security procedures for assessing electronic pollbook integrity.

BALLOT DESIGN

Overview and Analysis

The visual presentation of information on ballots has long been a topic of study. With regard to the presentation of information to voters, confidence in the outcome of elections is enhanced when ballots present information clearly and allow voters to make their selections in an intuitive way. Poor ballot design causes confusion and increases the possibility of a cast vote not reflecting the intention of the voter. Poor design may therefore threaten the accuracy of election results, since it may result in votes not cast as intended.

Ballot design requirements are often dictated by state law. Some states legislate the precise language that must be used on a ballot, and sometimes the exact design as well (e.g., layout or font size), making it difficult to update language or improve the functionality of the ballot over time. While there are some benefits to this prescriptive approach, it can hamper the implementation of new technology and introduce confusion for voters.

Ballot designs vary widely and depend on the voting machine or technology in use. Ballots can look different on different machines. Some ballots, like California's, are typically very long because they may include many statewide offices and initiatives. Initiatives are accompanied by short explanatory text which further extends the length of the ballot.

Poor ballot design can occur when election administrators fail to incorporate proven design principles or are constrained from doing so by voting technology features or local laws and regulations. Problems arise when a typeface is too small, the layout of the ballot is confusing, or the proper place or method to mark the voter's choice is difficult to discern. Poor ballot design has led to overvoting (inadvertently voting for more than one candidate for the same office), undervoting (failing to vote for any candidate in a contest), and mistaken selections. If, in the latter case, a voter attempts to strike out the erroneous vote and indicate an alternate choice, the ballot may be spoiled.

Two well-known examples of poor ballot design originated in Florida. The Palm Beach County "butterfly ballot" (see Figure 4-1) from the 2000 presidential election provides an example of how confusing ballot design can lead to miscast votes. The two-page ballot presented candidate names staggered on alternate sides of a central punch button column. The design directly contributed to an increased number of miscast votes in the election.[71] The 2006 general election ballot from Sarasota County illustrates how poor electronic ballot design (see Figure 4-2) may have caused many voters to overlook a congressional race.

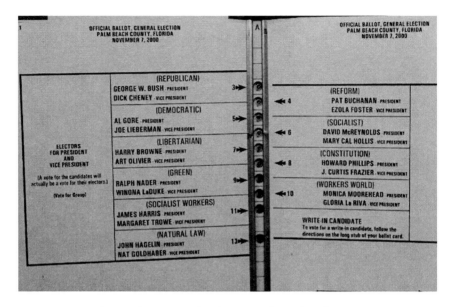

FIGURE 4-1 Palm Beach County, Florida "Butterfly Ballot" from 2000 presidential election.
SOURCE: https://commons.wikimedia.org/wiki/File:Butterfly_Ballot,_Florida_2000_(large).jpg. Image is ineligible for copyright and therefore in the public domain because it consists entirely of information that is common property and contains no original authorship.

---

[71] See Wand, Jonathan N., et al., "The Butterfly Did It: The Aberrant Vote for Buchanan in Palm Beach County, Florida," *The American Political Science Review*, December 2001, Vol. 95, No. 4, pp. 793-810.

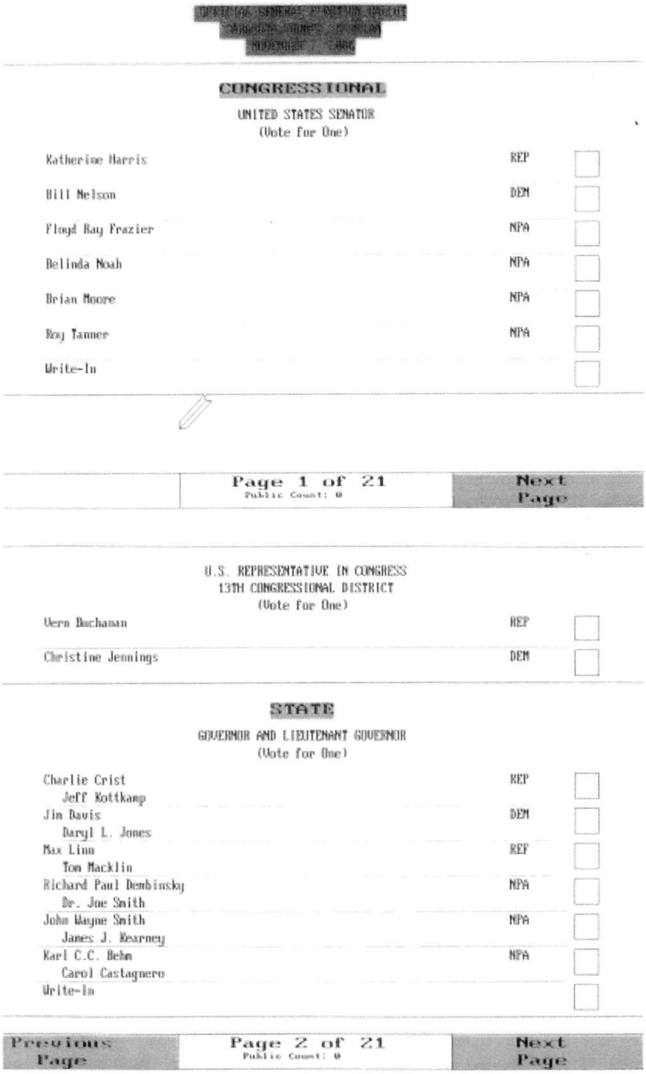

FIGURE 4-2 Sarasota County, Florida electronic ballot from 2006 general election. The congressional race on page 2 may seem to be a continuation of the Senate race on the previous page, as it appears between two major statewide races, both of which are introduced by large, colored headings. The congressional race does not have such a heading.

SOURCE: Jefferson, David, "What Happened in Sarasota County?," *The Bridge*, 2007, Vol. 37, No. 2, pp. 21-22. Reprinted with permission from Jefferson (2007).

BOX 4-1
Ballot Design and the Disabled Community

Careful ballot design is especially important with respect to disabled voters. Paper ballots in particular can present special challenges for disabled voters. Most paper ballots do not provide full accessibility and verification capacity to voters with visual impairments. While there are technological solutions that can make paper more accessible (e.g., audio input for review and instructions), good, accessibility-focused electronic ballot design is as critical as good physical paper ballot design. A poorly designed audio ballot can be more confusing than a poorly designed printed ballot.

On Election Day, it can be difficult to train voters to cast a vote if procedures are not readily apparent. Votes are cast on machines that may be accessed only briefly every year or two and voters have only minutes to read and mark their ballots. Good ballot design principles are essential when electronic displays are used to present ballots on voting equipment and ballot-marking devices. Studies show that 43 percent of otherwise literate Americans (93 million people) encounter difficulty reading ballot instructions.[72] Greater than 60 percent of Americans older than age 65 have physical disabilities that make reading or hearing instructions difficult.[73]

The use of ballot-marking devices (BMDs) is increasing, as paper ballots present special challenges for disabled voters (see Box 4-1).

Findings

Poor ballot design can significantly affect the ability of voters to understand the choices presented as well as voters' ability to make selections that reflect their intent.

Poorly designed ballots continue to be used in elections. The embedding of specific ballot design criteria into statutes and regulations makes it difficult to counteract poor design principles.

Ballot design can help voters be successful if it follows proven com-

---

[72] Quesenbery, Whitney, Center for Civic Design, presentation to the committee, June 13, 2017, New York, NY, citing U.S. Department of Education, Institute of Education Sciences, National Center for Education Statistics, National Assessment of Adult Literacy, 2003.

[73] Golden, Diane Cordry, Association of Assistive Technology Act Programs, presentation to the committee, June 13, 2017, New York, NY.

munication and display design principles to meet voters' needs for easy interaction, plain language, consistency, and comprehension.

Good designs for electronically displayed ballots (e.g., designs that foster interaction, facilitate navigation, and incorporate plain language) are positive contributors to the voting experience.

RECOMMENDATION

4.9   State requirements for ballot design (inclusive of print, screen, audio, etc.) and testing should use best practices developed by the U.S. Election Assistance Commission and other organizations with expertise in voter usability design (such as the Center for Civic Design).

VOTING TECHNOLOGY

Meeting requirements for cost-effective and accessible voting requires attention to a variety of factors including: (1) accuracy and security; (2) the structure of the election technology market; (3) technology innovation; (4) certification and standards; and (5) the capacity and capability of election administrators to oversee technology acquisition and maintenance.

Many elections today are dependent on electronic voting and vote tabulation systems that collect, store, and process votes. Most voting systems make use of computers and computer networks, but current cybersecurity and auditing requirements have placed increased value on paper even in the context of computerized systems.

As discussed previously, following the 2000 election, through HAVA, Congress provided funding for states to improve election systems. HAVA gave particular attention to statewide voter registration systems and to the procurement of voting systems that would eliminate the problems associated with mechanical lever machines and punch cards in the 2000 presidential election.

Requirements for today's voting systems include: (1) support for contemporary voting modes and innovative processes such as early voting and vote by mail; (2) usability; (3) accessibility for disabled voters; (4) enhanced cybersecurity; and (5) auditability.

The post-2000 modernization of voting technologies sought to redress deficiencies associated with ballot designs, eliminate punch card systems in which recounts had been plagued by hanging chad, and complete the phase-out of long-obsolete mechanical voting machines.

Jurisdictions that replaced punch card or lever machines generally adopted either optical-scan or Direct Recording Electronic (DRE) voting machines.

DREs generally take the form of a custom computer with a screen to display the ballot. Voters indicate their selections using a touchscreen or a physical keypad. DREs typically employ specialized software running on top of commodity operating systems like Windows or Linux and a mix of standard and custom hardware. In most systems, tabulated votes are recorded in a removable memory module. Some DREs can transmit ballots or vote totals to a central location for the reporting of unofficial results. DREs may be used in precincts on Election Day or in vote centers or during early voting.

Early in their existence, DREs were attractive to some election administrators because they provided a modern, reliable upgrade from mechanical lever machines. DREs seemed convenient to use, because they provided instant tabulation at the close of the polls, and because they eliminated the need to preprint the correct number of paper ballots for all the voters in each precinct.

HAVA directed jurisdictions responsible for federal elections to provide at least one accessible voting system at each polling place. DREs were widely embraced as a solution to the challenge of making voting accessible to the disabled, even in many jurisdictions that adopted optical scan balloting for nondisabled voters.

Although DREs successfully addressed several concerns, they also introduced new challenges. Critics pointed out cybersecurity risks inherent in relying entirely on computers—thereby eliminating a voter-inspected paper artifact that could be manually counted.[74] DREs also introduced new usability problems associated with how ballots are displayed on a screen, how users navigate within and across screens, and how voter selections are made. They also introduced new technical challenges; touchscreen miscalibration, for example, can cause a voter's intended vote for one candidate to be misinterpreted as a vote for another candidate.

The purchase of DREs may require a high initial investment. DREs require software updates and the ongoing payments for technical support costs. Furthermore, DREs introduced new complexities to the vote casting process and are subject to technological obsolescence.

Voting machines that create voter-verifiable paper audit trails (VVPATs) have been introduced to address some of these concerns. A VVPAT is a printout that provides a physical record of a voter's selections. VVPATs are preserved as a physical record of a cast ballot. While VVPATs provide a physical record of a cast ballot, it is possible that the information stored in a computer's memory does not reflect what is printed on the VVPAT.

---

[74] See, e.g., Jones, Douglas W. and Barbara Simons, *Broken Ballots: Will Your Votes Count?* (Chicago: University of Chicago Press, 2012) and Verified Voting Foundation, "The Resolution on Electronic Voting," available at: https://www.verifiedvotingfoundation.org/projects/electronic-voting-resolution/.

Voters may inspect a VVPAT to see whether it reflects their intended selections before their votes are recorded in computer memory. If voters do not verify that the information on their VVPAT is accurate, inaccuracies may be recorded. Those with vision or other impairments or limitations may not, however, be able to perform this inspection. Furthermore, it may be difficult to track patterns of VVPAT errors that would indicate fraud. Finally, a combined approach that uses DREs and printers introduces complexity and adds new points of potential failure at the polling place.

Jurisdictions typically transmit ballots to those wishing to cast ballots via mail. Ballots may sometimes be retrieved from an elections website for printing and completion by remote voters. Some jurisdictions may also provide remote voters with software to prepare their ballots. While this software avoids problems associated with manual use of paper ballots such as undervotes and overvotes and spoiled ballots (as voters get immediate feedback before completing their ballots), it introduces additional security risks. Completed ballots are returned via mail, at designated collection points, or, in certain instances, by fax or via the Internet.

Well designed, voter-marked paper ballots are the standard for usability for voters without disabilities. Research on VVPATs has shown that they are not usable/reliable for verifying that the ballot of record accurately reflects the voter's intent, but there is limited research on the usability of BMDs for this purpose. BMDs moreover, may produce either a full ballot, a summary ballot, or a "selections-only" ballot. Unless a voter takes notes while voting, BMDs that print only selections with abbreviated names/descriptions of the contests are virtually unusable for verifying voter intent.[75]

Human beings must, however, interact not only with ballots, but also with all components of election systems. A usability failure of any particular component of an election system can be as detrimental as a failure of usability in the ballot. A voting system must be usable in a way that allows a voter to verify that the ballot of record correctly reflects his or her intent. Vote tabulation systems must be usable in a way that facilitates the correct tallying and tabulation of votes. Auditing technology must be useable in a way that enables efficient recounting.

Findings

Not all voting systems have the capacity for the independent auditing of the results of vote casting. Electronic voting systems that do not produce

---

[75] By hand marking a paper ballot, a voter is, in essence, attending to the marks made on his or her ballot. A BMD-produced ballot need not be reviewed at all by the voter. Furthermore, it may be difficult to review a long or complex BMD-produced ballot. This has prompted calls for hand-marked (as opposed to BMD-produced) paper ballots whenever possible.

a human-readable paper ballot of record raise security and verifiability concerns.

The software for casting and tabulating votes is not uniformly independent in voting systems.

Voting technology raises a particular set of issues for the disabled community.

Additional research on ballots produced by BMDs will be necessary to understand the effectiveness of such ballots.

RECOMMENDATIONS

4.10 States and local jurisdictions should have policies in place for routine replacement of election systems.

4.11 Elections should be conducted with human-readable paper ballots. These may be marked by hand or by machine (using a ballot-marking device); they may be counted by hand or by machine (using an optical scanner).[76] Recounts and audits should be conducted by human inspection of the human-readable portion of the paper ballots. Voting machines that do not provide the capacity for independent auditing (e.g., machines that do not produce a voter-verifiable paper audit trail) should be removed from service as soon as possible.

4.12 Every effort should be made to use human-readable paper ballots in the 2018 federal election. All local, state, and federal elections should be conducted using human-readable paper ballots by the 2020 presidential election.

4.13 Computers and software used to prepare ballots (i.e., ballot-marking devices) should be separate from computers and software used to count and tabulate ballots (scanners). Voters should have an opportunity to review and confirm their selections before depositing the ballot for tabulation.

VOTING SYSTEM CERTIFICATION

Overview and Analysis

Under HAVA, the EAC became responsible for developing and administering a voluntary system for federal certification of voting systems.[77] These

---

[76] A modern form of optical scanner, a *digital scanner*, captures, interprets, and stores a high-resolution image of the voter's ballot at a resolution of 300 dots per inch (DPI) or higher.

[77] U.S. Election Assistance Commission, "Testing & Certification Program Manual, Version 2.0," available at: https://www.eac.gov/assets/1/6/Cert_Manual_7_8_15_FINAL.pdf.

guidelines, known as the Voluntary Voting System Guidelines (VVSG), specify certain functional, accessibility, and security requirements for voting systems.

The EAC has two responsibilities pertinent to certification. First, with the technical assistance of the National Institute of Standards and Technology (NIST), the EAC oversees the development of the VVSG, which establishes the standards against which new voting systems are tested. Second, the EAC certifies independent voting system testing laboratories (VSTLs), which conduct the testing of new voting systems developed by commercial vendors.

States are ultimately responsible for determining the process by which voting systems will be certified in their states. Thirty-eight states and the District of Columbia rely on the federal testing and certification program, at least to some extent.[78] This can range from requiring that systems be tested to federal standards to requiring that systems be tested in federally approved laboratories. The remaining states do not require federal testing or certification per se, but in most cases rely on the federal certification program to guide their own state certification regimes. HAVA envisioned that the states might also perform testing of the accuracy, usability, and durability of the systems that they proposed to put into service.

The federal certification process begins only once a manufacturer has registered with the EAC Voting System Testing and Certification Program and has submitted a system for certification.[79] The process of certification can take up to 2 years. [80] Even then, a state certification process frequently follows after federal certification has been received. Following certification, other procedures, such as acceptance testing, logic and accuracy testing, and special purpose tests may follow. All told, the period between the develop-

---

[78] See National Conference of State Legislatures, "Voting System Standards, Testing, and Certification," available at: http://www.ncsl.org/research/elections-and-campaigns/voting-system-standards-testing-and-certification.aspx.

[79] See "Testing & Certification Program Manual, Version 2.0." Systems are usually "submitted when (1) they are new to the marketplace, (2) they have never before received an EAC certification, (3) they are modified, or (4) the Manufacturer wishes to test a previously certified system to a different (newer) standard." See p. 19.

[80] Perez, Eddie, Hart InterCivic and Coutts, McDermot, Unisys Voting Solutions, presentations to the committee, December 8, 2017, Denver, CO. See also University of Pennsylvania, Wharton Public Policy Initiative, "The Business of Voting: Market Structure and Innovation in the Election Technology Industry," 2016, p. 38, available at: https://publicpolicy.wharton.upenn.edu/live/files/270-the-business-of-voting.

ment of a new voting systems and its actual use in an election can last years and cost vendors millions of dollars.[81]

Current security standards certify equipment but not associated procedures and procedural requirements (e.g., auditing). This fact contributes to deficiencies in current standards.

Newly revised voluntary voting system guidelines, called VVSG 2.0, await final approval from the EAC. The new guidelines provide a more modular set of specifications and requirements against which voting systems can be tested to determine whether the systems provide basic functional, accessibility, and security capabilities required of these systems. This change is intended to foster the deployment of accurate and secure voting systems while also enabling system innovation that would allow the deployment of system upgrades in a timely fashion, facilitate interoperability of election systems, permit the transparent assessment of the performance of election systems, and provide a set of testable requirements that are easy to use and understand.[82] The approach of VVSG 2.0 focuses more on functional requirements than on the prescriptive specifics of the past. The draft guidelines require software independence for all voting systems in order to allow the correct outcome of an election to be determined even if the software does not perform as intended.[83,84]

Findings

Vendors and election administrators have expressed frustration with the certification process as presently implemented.

Costs and delays in the certification process may limit vendor innovation and increase system costs.

The requirements of the certification system can create barriers to

---

[81] The software used in voting systems is also subject to certification. This has important implications for system security. If the most recent version of particular software has not been certified, states may be forced to use an earlier software version with documented vulnerabilities.

[82] U.S. Election Assistance Commission, "VVSG Version 2.0: Scope and Structure," available at: https://www.eac.gov/assets/1/6/VVSGv_2_0_Scope-Structure(DRAFTv_8).pdf.

[83] "A voting system is software independent if an (undetected) change or error in its software cannot cause an undetectable change or error in an election outcome." See Rivest, Ronald L., "On the Notion of 'Software Independence' in Voting Systems," *Philosophical Transactions of the Royal Society A*, October 28, 2008, DOI: 10.1098/rsta.2008.0149. Dr. Rivest is a member of the committee that authored the current report.

An auditable voting system is software independent.

[84] The auditing of election results can reduce the need for certification and simultaneously provide better evidence that outcomes are correct. See, e.g., Stark, Philip B. and David A. Wagner, "Evidence-Based Elections," *IEEE Security and Privacy*, 2012, Vol. 10, DOI 10.1109/MSP.2012.62.

incremental improvements to systems that reflect improved manufacturing processes or software upgrades. This contributes to the process that has created a population of voting systems that have become obsolete (and therefore harder to secure) when compared even to the technology one encounters in today's typical office environment.

New approaches to the standards-setting and certification process (i.e., VVSG 2.0) have the potential to mitigate deficiencies in the current system.

RECOMMENDATIONS

4.14 If the principles and guidelines of the final Voluntary Voting System Guidelines are consistent with those proposed in September 2017, they should be adopted by the U.S. Election Assistance Commission.

4.15 Congress should:

  a. authorize and fund the U.S. Election Assistance Commission to develop voluntary certification standards for voter registration databases, electronic pollbooks, chain-of-custody procedures, and auditing; and

  b. provide the funding necessary to sustain the U.S. Election Assistance Commission's Voluntary Voting System Guidelines standard-setting process and certification program.

4.16 The U.S. Election Assistance Commission and the National Institute of Standards and Technology should continue the process of refining and improving the Voluntary Voting System Guidelines to reflect changes in how elections are administered, to respond to new challenges to election systems (e.g., cyberattacks), and to take advantage of opportunities as new technologies become available.

4.17 Strong cybersecurity standards should be incorporated into the standards-setting and certification processes at the federal and state levels.

5

Ensuring the Integrity of Elections

In this chapter, the committee discusses threats to the integrity of U.S.
elections. Two topics that play critical roles in protecting this integrity,
cybersecurity and auditing, are considered. The committee then assesses
the widely proposed suggestion that ballots be cast via the Internet.

INTRODUCTION

There are numerous ways in which the integrity of elections can be
affected. Election results may be improperly tallied or reported. Inaccuracies may be introduced by human error or because of a lack of proper
oversight. Vote counts can be affected if fraudulent voting, e.g., multiple
voting, illegal voting, etc., occurs. Election tallies and reporting may also
be affected by malicious actors.

Malicious actors can affect vote counts by:

- introducing inaccuracies in the recording, maintenance, and tallying of votes; and/or
- altering or destroying evidence necessary to audit and verify the
correct reporting of election results.[1]

There are many ways to prevent the casting of votes. Voters can be
physically barred or otherwise deterred (e.g., by intimidation) from access-

---

[1] Other threats, e.g., disinformation campaigns, gerrymandering, etc., may affect election
integrity and, while important, were viewed by the committee as outside of its charge.

ing polling sites. Information on voting locations, voting times, and voting processes may be manipulated to mislead potential voters. Disruptions in mail or Internet service may adversely affect remote voters. Registration data may be altered to disenfranchise voters. Voting equipment failures or inadequate supplies could prevent vote collection.

After votes have been cast, physical or electronic ballots can be altered, destroyed, or lost. Counting errors may affect manual or electronic tallying methods. Tallies may be inaccurately reported because of carelessness or malicious activity.

After the primary reporting of results, evidence that enables verification of the reported results may be altered or destroyed. This evidence could include original artifacts (e.g., cast ballots) or supplemental data provided to enable external auditing and verification.

Disruptions of Electronic Systems

Security vulnerabilities can be exploited to electronically disrupt voting or affect vote counts at polling locations or in instances of remote voting.

Denial-of-service Attacks

Denial-of-service (DoS) attacks interrupt or slow access to computer systems.[2] DoS can be used to disrupt vote casting, vote tallying, or election audits by preventing access to e-pollbooks, electronic voting systems, or electronic auditing systems.

When employed against even a limited number of jurisdictions, DoS disruptions could lead to a loss in confidence in overall election integrity. A DoS attack targeting select jurisdictions could alter the outcome of an election.

Malware

Malware—malicious software that includes worms, spyware, viruses, Trojan horses, and ransomware—is perhaps the greatest threat to electronic voting.[3] Malware can be introduced at any point in the electronic path of a

---

[2] If equipment is manipulated to slow its operation or compromise its operability, this may also constitute a DoS attack.

[3] Worms are standalone computer programs that replicate themselves in order to spread to other computers, possibly compromising the operability of the computers they infect now or in the future. Spyware is software that aims to gather information about a person or organization without their knowledge, that may send such information to another entity without the consumer's consent, or that asserts control over a device without the consumer's knowledge. A computer virus is a type of malicious software program that, when executed, replicates

vote—from the software behind the vote-casting interface to the software tabulating votes—to prevent a voter's vote from being recorded as intended.

Malware can prevent voting by compromising or disrupting e-pollbooks or by disabling vote-casting systems. It can prevent correct tallying by altering or destroying electronic records or by causing software to miscount electronic ballots or physical ballots (e.g., in instances where optical scanners are used in the vote tabulation process). Malware can also be used to disrupt auditing software.

Malware is not easily detected. It can be introduced into systems via software updates, removable media with ballot definition files, and through the exploitation of software errors in networked systems. It may also be introduced by direct physical access, e.g., by individuals operating inappropriately at points during the manufacturing of the election system or at the level of elections offices. It is difficult to comprehensively thwart the introduction of malware in all these instances.

Other Classes of Attacks

There are other avenues through which electronic systems may be disrupted. Malicious actors may obtain sensitive information such as usernames or passwords by pretending to be a trustworthy entity in an electronic communication. Servers may be breached to obtain administrator-level credentials. Individuals with site access (e.g., employees or contractors) might physically access a system.

Maintaining Voter Anonymity

If anonymity is compromised, voters may not express their true preferences. Anonymity can be compromised in many ways. Clandestine cameras at poll sites could be used to compromise voter anonymity. Latent fingerprints left on ballots might be used to link voters to their ballots. Full ballots dissociated from individual voters might be posted in the interest of ensuring transparency and/or to facilitate auditing, but it may be possible to tie particular ballots to individual voters. When voter anonymity is achieved using encryption, a failure in the encryption can lead to the disclosure of a voter's identity. With remote voting—voting outside of publicly monitored poll sites—it may not be difficult to compromise voter privacy. When voting, for example, by mail, fax, or via the Internet, individuals can

---

itself by modifying other computer programs and inserting its own code. Trojan horses are malicious computer programs that mislead users of their true intent. Ransomware is a type of malicious software that threatens to publish the victim's data or perpetually block access to it unless a ransom is paid.

be coerced or paid to vote for particular candidates outside the oversight of election administrators.

ELECTION CYBERSECURITY

Overview and Analysis

As described in Chapter 1, the Help America Vote Act (HAVA) prompted the acceleration of the introduction of electronic systems throughout the U.S. election process. There have since been concerns about vulnerabilities in the electronic systems that are used to perform most election functions. Given competing demands for attention and resources, these concerns have not always been a high priority for election administrators. However, citizen and government attention to these vulnerabilities greatly increased following reports of Russian efforts to compromise voter registration systems during the 2016 presidential election.

Attention brought to the problem of election cybersecurity during the 2016 election prompted energetic reactions from government, academia, and the public and private sectors. Following the U.S. Department of Homeland Security (DHS) designation of elections as critical national infrastructure, election administrators established the Elections Infrastructure Information Sharing and Analysis Center (EI-ISAC) to improve information sharing among election officials. In addition, governmental and private-sector coordinating councils were established to share information and engage with DHS to address cyber threats to elections. In addition, organizations such as the Center for Internet Security and the Belfer Center at Harvard University have issued guides and "playbooks" to assist state and local officials in the mitigation of risks to their electronic system and in the adoption of best security practices.[4] Most recently, as part of the omnibus FY 2018 appropriations bill, the U.S. Congress appropriated $380 million "to the Election Assistance Commission for necessary expenses to make payments to States for activities to improve the administration of elections for Federal office, including to enhance election technology and make election security improvements."[5]

Election administrators face a daunting task in responding to cyber threats, as cybersecurity is a concern with all computer systems. This is

---

[4] See The Center for Internet Security, "A Handbook for Elections Infrastructure Security," available at: https://www.cisecurity.org/elections-resources/, and Belfer Center for Science and International Affairs, Harvard Kennedy School, "The State and Local Election Cybersecurity Playbook," available at: https://www.belfercenter.org/publication/state-and-local-election-cybersecurity-playbook.

[5] See H.R. 1625, Consolidated Appropriations Act, 2018, Section 501, available at: https://www.congress.gov/bill/115th-congress/house-bill/1625/text.

because (1) the design and development of current computer systems, no matter how well constructed, cannot anticipate and prevent all the possible means of attack; and (2) there are parties that will act in deliberately hostile ways to exploit vulnerabilities.

Vulnerabilities arise because of the complexity of modern information technology (IT) systems and human fallibility in making judgments about what actions are safe or unsafe from a cybersecurity perspective. Moreover, cybersecurity is a never-ending challenge. It is unlikely that permanent protections against cyber threats will be developed in the near future given that cybersecurity threats evolve and that adversaries continually adopt new techniques to compromise systems or overcome defenses. The general view is that the offense has the upper hand if the attacker is patient and well resourced. With respect to foreign threats, the challenge is compounded by the great asymmetry between the capabilities and resources available to local jurisdictions in the United States and those of foreign intelligence services.

Unfortunately, not all vendors or jurisdictions follow established best practices with respect to the development, maintenance, and operation of voting systems. This makes them more vulnerable to cyber-manipulation than they need to be. In comparison with other sectors (e.g., banking), many jurisdictions in the election sector are not following best security practices with regard to cybersecurity, one reason being that the banking industry is highly regulated, and part of these regulations is the supervision of their cybersecurity strategies.[6]

Several factors affect a bad actor's ability to compromise a system: (1) how well the system was designed; (2) whether the system is properly configured and updated; (3) how well the system is managed and operated; and (4) the skills, resources, and determination of the would-be attacker. Adoption of best practices for developing, testing, and management of systems can reduce (but not eliminate) the risk of a successful cyberattack. As a rule, stronger defenses increase the time and effort required to conduct an attack, and well-defended targets are less attractive to would-be attackers.

There are many layers between the application software that implements an electoral function and the transistors inside the computers that ultimately carry out computations. These layers include the election application itself (e.g., for voter registration or vote tabulation); the user interface; the application runtime system; the operating system (e.g., Linux or Windows); the system bootloader (e.g., BIOS or UEFI); the microprocessor firmware (e.g., Intel Management Engine); disk drive firmware; system-on-

---

[6] See, e.g., https://www.occ.treas.gov/news-issuances/news-releases/2017/nr-occ-2017-113.html and https://www.csbs.org/sites/default/files/2017-11/CSBS%20Cybersecurity%20101%20Resource%20Guide%20FINAL.pdf.

chip firmware; and the microprocessor's microcode. For this reason, it is difficult to know for certain whether a system has been compromised by malware. One might inspect the application-layer software and confirm that it is present on the system's hard drive, but any one of the layers listed above, if hacked, may substitute a fraudulent application layer (e.g., vote-counting software) at the time that the application is supposed to run. As a result, there is no technical mechanism that can ensure that every layer in the system is unaltered and thus no technical mechanism that can ensure that a computer application will produce accurate results. This has several important implications for election systems:

- all digital information—such as ballot definitions, voter choice records, vote tallies, or voter registration lists—is subject to malicious alteration;
- there is no technical mechanism currently available that can ensure that a computer application—such as one used to record or count votes—will produce accurate results;
- testing alone cannot ensure that systems have not been compromised; and
- any computer system used for elections—such as a voting machine or e-pollbook—can be rendered inoperable.

Election systems are especially vulnerable when they are connected to the Internet, telephone network,[7] or another wide-area network.[8] Systems that utilize network connections for their functions include voter registration systems, e-pollbooks, and post-election canvassing/reporting systems.

Even when systems are not directly connected to networks, they are vulnerable to attack through physical or wireless access.[9] They also are vulnerable whenever data transferred to them originates from another computer system that is itself vulnerable. For example, to attack a voting machine that receives data only through hand-carried removable media bearing "ballot definition files," an attacker might create a ballot definition file that takes advantage of a flaw in the software that reads a ballot definition file or displays a ballot.[10] Such an attacker need not be physically

---

[7] The telephone network is actually now part of the Internet. Land-line switching centers and cell-phone towers connect to each other through packet-switched networks (i.e., the technology underlying the Internet) that are connected to the larger Internet via border routers.

[8] Most wide-area networks are also connected to the larger Internet.

[9] Attacks are possible not only when systems are in use for elections but also during the manufacturing process or when such systems are in transit or in storage.

[10] Essentially every type of electronic voting machine must be programmed with ballot designs shortly before an election. As such, this is a particularly tempting attack vector, particularly for sophisticated actors.

present with that removable media—entry through a network-connected computer that creates the removable storage media may suffice (the removable storage media is used to transmit the ballot definition file).

Achieving stronger defenses against cyberattacks involves: (1) adopting state-of-the-art technologies and best practices more widely; and (2) developing new knowledge about cybersecurity. The first defense is primarily nontechnical and involves economic, organizational, and behavioral factors. The second defense requires research to develop new technologies and approaches.[11]

Cybersecurity and Vote Tabulation

Because there is no realistic mechanism to fully secure vote casting and tabulation computer systems from cyber threats, one must adopt methods that can assure the accuracy of the election outcome without relying on the hardware and software used to conduct the election. Uniform adoption of auditing best practices does not prevent tampering with the results collected and tabulated by computers. It can allow such tampering to be detected and often corrected. Good auditing practices can demonstrate that the results of an election accurately reflect the intention of the electorate without a need to trust the equipment used to conduct the election.

Cybersecurity and E-pollbooks

With respect to e-pollbooks and other election systems used during the election, independent backup systems are necessary in the event that primary systems become unavailable. E-pollbook data have traditionally been backed up with paper printouts. As an alternative, databases might be stored on static media such as DVDs. However, in jurisdictions that offer same-day registration or convenience voting in self-selected locations, relying on paper could lead to new risks of in-person voter fraud.[12] Addressing this risk by building fully independent systems (including independent networks connecting the polling sites) is not practical.[13]

---

[11] National Research Council, *At the Nexus of Cybersecurity and Public Policy: Some Basic Concepts and Issues* (National Academies Press, Washington DC: 2014).

[12] While paper pollbooks will not proactively stop some forms of multiple voting, their use permits the retroactive detection of such activity and provides evidence against those acting illegally.

[13] In practice, there is no such thing as an independent network. See, e.g., footnote 7.

Factors that Exacerbate Cybersecurity Concerns

- *A highly decentralized elections system.* Because the U.S. elections system is highly decentralized, responsibility for cybersecurity often falls to the county or municipal level where expertise and resources may be quite limited.
- *Aging systems.* Because U.S. elections frequently make use of hardware and software that are aging—in some cases to the point that they would generally be considered obsolete—cybersecurity risk is increased because (1) such systems may fall well behind the current state of the art in cybersecurity measures; and (2) software or the operating system used to run it may no longer be receiving security updates.
- *Changing threat.* Traditionally, the goal has been to secure against election fraud by corrupt candidates or their supporters who may attempt to favor a particular candidate by altering or destroying votes or tampering with the vote tally. The 2016 election vividly illustrated that hostile state actors can also pose a threat. These actors often possess more sophisticated capabilities and can apply greater resources to the conduct of such operations. Moreover, they may have other goals than shifting the outcome for a particular candidate. If their goal is to disrupt an election or undermine confidence in its outcome, they may need only to achieve DoS against e-pollbooks or leave behind traces of interference like malicious software or evidence of tampering with voter registration lists or other records. Even failed attempts at interference could, if detected, cast doubt on the validity of election results absent robust mechanisms to detect and recover from such attacks.

Findings

There is no realistic mechanism to fully secure vote casting and tabulation computer systems from cyber threats.

U.S. elections are conducted using systems that are aging and prone to security vulnerabilities and operational failures. The continued use of outdated systems increases the possibility of a critical failure. Even if actual failures or compromises do not occur, there is a risk that public confidence in the electoral process could be undermined by the possibility of such compromise—especially if there are indications that such a compromise was attempted.

In comparison with other sectors (e.g., banking), the election sector is not following best security practices with regard to cybersecurity.

Data discrepancies are more difficult to detect in elections than in most other sectors because voters do not generally learn whether their votes were processed correctly.[14]

Even if best practices are applied, systems will not be completely secure. Foreign state–sponsored attacks present a challenge for even the most responsible and well-resourced jurisdictions. Small, under-resourced jurisdictions are at serious risk.

Appropriate audits can be used to enable trust in the accuracy of election outcomes even if the integrity of software, hardware, personnel, or other aspects of the system on which an election is run were to be questioned.

Better cybersecurity is not a substitute for effective auditing.

RECOMMENDATIONS

5.1   Election systems should continue to be considered as U.S. Department of Homeland Security–designated critical infrastructure.

5.2   The U.S. Election Assistance Commission and U.S. Department of Homeland Security should continue to develop and maintain a detailed set of cybersecurity best practices for state and local election officials. Election system vendors and state and local election officials should incorporate these best practices into their operations.

5.3   The U.S. Election Assistance Commission should closely monitor the expenditure of funds made available to the states for election security through the 2018 omnibus appropriations bill to ensure that the funds enhance security practices and do not simply replace local dollars with federal support for ongoing activities.[15] The U.S. Election Assistance Commission should closely monitor any future federal funding designated to enhance election security.

5.4   Congress should provide funding for state and local governments to improve their cybersecurity capabilities on an ongoing basis.

ELECTION AUDITING

Overview and Analysis

Election audits are critical to ensuring the integrity of election outcomes and for raising voter confidence. Auditing can demonstrate the validity of

---

[14] End-to-end-verifiable systems have the capacity to demonstrate to voters that their votes were properly counted.

[15] See H.R. 1625, Consolidated Appropriations Act, 2018, Section 501, available at: https://www.congress.gov/bill/115th-congress/house-bill/1625/text.

an election outcome and provide an indication of errors in ballot tabulation. Effective auditing contributes to voting security by providing an answer to the question, "Can we trust the outcome of an election when the equipment (hardware and software) used to conduct the election may have vulnerabilities or when the process is subject to human error?"

For decades, traditional audits have been performed (and have been required by law) in many states. While election administrators have performed many types of post-election audits, such as process audits, the most widely known audits have been audits of cast ballots. Traditional ballot auditing requires that election results in some fixed percentage of precincts be reconfirmed by a hand count—though the details of actual implementation can reduce the value of the audit (election administrators should not, for example, always audit the same precincts).

Hand counting every ballot cast to be certain of the outcome is extremely time-consuming, and hand counts are susceptible to error or deliberate miscounting. The use of computerized voting machines provides flexibility and processing efficiencies. Nevertheless, computers are, as was discussed in the previous section, subject to programming errors, manipulation, and outside interference. Election audits have, therefore, become more important, as the performance of audits raises voter confidence in the reported outcomes of elections. The use of networked communication at various election stages has necessitated audits that address cybersecurity risks.

An evidence-based election would produce not only a reported (or initial) election outcome, but also evidence that the reported outcome is correct. This evidence may be examined in a "recount" or in a "post-election audit" to provide assurance that the reported outcome indeed is the result of a correct tabulation of cast ballots.

Voter-verifiable paper ballots provide a simple form of such evidence provided that many voters have verified their ballots. The ability of each voter to verify that a paper ballot correctly records his or her choices, before the ballot is cast, means that the collection of cast paper ballots forms a body of evidence that is not subject to manipulation by faulty hardware or software. These cast paper ballots may be recounted after the election or may be selectively examined by hand in a post-election audit. Such an evidence trail is generally preferred over electronic evidence like electronic cast-vote records or ballot images. Electronic evidence can be altered by compromised or faulty hardware or software.

Paper ballots are designed to provide a human-readable recording of a voter's choices. The term "paper ballot" here refers to a "voter-verifiable paper ballot," in the sense that voters have the opportunity to verify that their choices are correctly recorded before they cast their paper ballots. The voter may mark the ballot by hand, or the marked ballot may be produced by a voting machine. In the current context, the human-readable portion of the paper ballot is the official ballot of record that acts as the record of the voter's expressed choices.[16] Any human-readable, durable, tamper-evident medium such as cloth, cardstock, or plastic could be used instead of paper.

Statistical auditing techniques available now (and some in development) are more efficient and effective than earlier techniques wherein a predetermined percentage of precincts were recounted by hand to confirm the accuracy of initial precinct tallies. The implementation of statistical auditing techniques may require the allocation of additional time between the end of voting and when the official results of the election are certified.

Risk-Limiting Auditing

Auditing a fixed percentage of precincts may not provide adequate assurance with regard to the outcome of a close election. To address this weakness, a method of auditing known as risk-limiting auditing was developed.[17] Risk-limiting audits (RLAs) operate dynamically by examining individual randomly selected paper ballots until sufficient statistical assurance is obtained. This statistical assurance ensures that the chance that an incorrect reported outcome escapes detection and correction is less than a predetermined risk limit.

RLAs offer statistical efficiency. Auditing an election with tens of millions of ballots may require examining by hand as few as several hundred randomly selected paper ballots. A RLA might determine that more ballots need to be examined, or even that a full hand recount should be performed, if the contest is close or the reported outcome incorrect. Because RLAs layer a security mechanism (the risk-limiting audit itself) on top of the traditional vote-casting process, RLAs can often be performed without the adoption of new vote-casting processes. RLAs were piloted statewide in Colorado in 2017 and are now being piloted by several other states.[18]

---

[16] Rather than, for example, an electronic interpretation of the paper ballot or a non-human-readable barcode appearing on a ballot.

[17] For a general discussion of risk-limiting audits, see Lindeman, Mark and Philip B. Stark, "A Gentle Introduction to Risk-limiting Audits," *IEEE Security and Privacy*, Special Issue on Electronic Voting, 2012.

[18] The changes required to implement risk-limiting audits incur costs and require detailed planning, education, and development of required resources. Some states will, for example, need to adopt paper balloting (or purchase different scanners to be able to use comparison-based audits).

Executing an RLA for a single plurality contest in a single jurisdiction is not particularly challenging. Implementing an RLA for an election with multiple contests, multiple jurisdictions, multiple types of equipment, and multiple election types (not just plurality), requires more preparation, and a state (or other jurisdiction) should expect that the implementation process will take time.

The most efficient RLAs (comparison audits) make use of cast-vote records (CVRs) that electronically represent the contents of each paper ballot. A ballot-comparison audit operates by randomly selecting paper ballots from a list of all cast paper ballots on a ballot manifest and comparing the voter-verified human-readable contents of the selected paper ballots to the electronic records in the corresponding CVRs. When CVRs are not available (or cannot be linked to specific corresponding paper ballots), a ballot-polling audit may be used instead when margins are relatively large. Such an audit examines only randomly selected paper ballots (and no CVRs); however, many more paper ballots may need to be sampled and examined to achieve the same statistical assurance.[19]

RLAs can establish high confidence in the accuracy of election results—even if the equipment that produced the original tallies is faulty. This confidence depends on two conditions: (1) that election administrators follow appropriate procedures to maintain the chain-of-custody and secure physical ballots—from the time ballots are received, either in-person or by mail, until auditing is complete; and (2) that the personnel conducting the audit are following appropriate auditing procedures and the equipment and software used to audit the election are independent of the equipment and software used to produce the initial tallies. In the latter case, this not only requires that the software be independent of the software used to tally votes, but also that the software's specifications/algorithms, inputs, and outputs are transparent to permit members of the public to reproduce the software's operation.

End-to-end-verifiability

In recent years there has been increased interest in providing voters with an opportunity to verify that their votes have been accurately cast, counted, and tabulated. This presents a challenge due to the necessity of preserving the secrecy of the ballot. However, building upon cryptographic methods initially developed by computer scientist and cryptographer David Lee Chaum, researchers have developed an approach called end-to-end (E2E) verifiability. This approach enables voters and other members of the

---

In Colorado, the cost to the state to conduct its pilot of RLAs was $90,000 (Hall, Hilary, Boulder County (CO) Clerk and Recorder, presentation to committee, December 7, 2017, Denver, CO). Free & Fair, which developed the open-source tools used to conduct the Colorado RLA invested an additional $100,000 in the effort (Kiniry, Joe, Free & Fair, presentation to committee, December 7, 2017, Denver, CO).

[19] Not all optical scanners can produce CVRs that can be linked to specific paper ballots; linked CVR–based RLAs are more efficent and cost-effective than ballot-polling RLAs; therefore, the ability to produce linked CVRs is an important consideration when purchasing and deploying voting machines.

public to audit the integrity of an election without relying on hardware, software, or personnel associated with elections.[20]

An election is E2E-verifiable (E2E-V) if it achieves three goals: 1) voters can obtain assurance that their selections have been properly recorded; 2) any individual can verify that his or her ballots have been included in vote tallies; and 3) members of the public can verify that the final tally is the correct result for the set of ballots collected. E2E-verifiability enables not only detection of external threats, but also detection of internal threats including errors or tampering by election officials, corrupted equipment, or compromises originating with equipment vendors.

E2E-V voting systems adopt certain properties (see Box 5-1), encrypt ballot data, and permit verification of data throughout the voting process. In an election context, "end-to-end" refers to the flow of ballot data through the entirety of the voting process and to the idea that the data may be verified at multiple stages in the voting process. The phrase should not, however, be interpreted to mean that verification must occur at particular stages of the process.

E2E-verifiability is a property that may be achieved in an election—rather than a particular methodology. Systems with various characteristics have been designed to produce E2E-V elections. In practice, an E2E-V voting system might work as follows:

Upon marking a ballot, the voter would obtain a receipt which is a "cryptographically-masked" copy of the voter's selections (the voter's choices would thus not be visible in a way that would enable vote-selling or coercion). The receipt could be machine-issued or derived from the process of marking a pre-printed paper ballot.

There are several methods to test whether the encryption process is working properly. In one scenario, voters might be allowed to "spoil" one or more ballots after receipts have been produced.[21] Voters could subsequently verify that receipts issued for spoiled ballots accurately reflect selections made. Because voting systems cannot predict whether a voter

---

[20] For a general discussion of end-to-end (E2E) election verifiability, see Benaloh, Josh, et. al, "End-to-end Verifiability," 2014, available at: https://pdfs.semanticscholar.org/4650/db843e0e90ca7ff54c7fe8e6080d12f6a0fc.pdf. Dr. Benaloh is a member of the committee that authored the current report. Dr. Ronald L. Rivest, who is also a member of the committee that authored the current report, was a co-author of the paper and has authored other papers on end-to-end verifiability.

[21] A *spoiled ballot* is a ballot that is invalidated and not included in the vote tally. Ballots might be spoiled accidentally or deliberately. A ballot may be spoiled in many ways (e.g., if the ballot is defaced, if invalidating stray marks are added to the ballot, etc.).

Voters would be permitted to verify the accuracy of the encryption only on spoiled ballots. This is to ensure that the verification process could not be used to reveal how individuals actually voted.

BOX 5-1
Properties of End-to-end-verifiable Voting Systems

End-to-end-verifiable (E2E-V) voting systems share the following security properties:

Integrity. Once a voter successfully enters his or her ballot into an E2E-V system, it cannot be undetectably lost or modified in any way, even in the presence of computer bugs or malicious logic.

Counting Accuracy. Ballots cannot be miscounted without the miscount being detectable.

Public Verifiability. E2E-V systems provide outputs and publish sufficient verification data to permit any voter to verify that his or her ballot was not lost or modified and that votes were properly tabulated. Verification data provides cryptographic proof that ballot integrity was preserved and tabulation was correct. Anyone may run a verification program on the verification data to confirm the accuracy of the data.

Transparency. Mathematical principles underlying the E2E-V security guarantees are open and public. The specifications for verification programs are publicly documented, and voters and observers are free to create and execute their own verification programs.

SOURCE: Adapted from U.S. Vote Foundation, "The Future of Voting: End-to-end Verifiable Internet Voting," July 2015, p. 111, available at: https://www.usvotefoundation.org/sites/default/files/E2EVIV_full_report.pdf.
Dr. Ronald L. Rivest and Dr. Josh Benaloh, members of the committee that authored the current report, made contributions to the U.S. Vote Foundation report.

will spoil a ballot, a voting system must correctly encrypt all receipts, as only a small fraction of voters would need to verify that spoiled ballots have been properly encrypted to reveal systematic erroneous behavior by a voting system.

After polls close, copies of all voter receipts would be posted to a public electronic bulletin board in order to allow voters to confirm that their votes have been properly recorded. If the voter's unique receipt was not posted, the voter could file a protest and use the receipt as evidence for correcting the posting error.

All voter receipts would be processed using a series of cryptographic computations that would yield the results of the particular election. The algorithms and parameters for the cryptographic operations would be posted on a website to enable voters to verify that their votes were tallied as recorded and to allow other observers to verify that the tally is correct.[22]

When E2E-verifiability is used with paper ballots, conventional recounts and risk-limiting audits are possible as additional means of verification.

E2E-verifiablility adds complexity to the election process, and the effective wide-scale deployment of E2E-verifiability will require a broad understanding of the underlying cryptographic methods by election officials and the general public. It may initially be challenging to understand the tools that could be employed to make E2E-verifiability possible.[23] Further, with E2E-V systems, it is possible that the encryption of voter receipts could be compromised. While such decryption would not affect the integrity of an election, it could compromise voter anonymity.

E2E-V methods seem to be necessary for secure voting via the Internet, but the methods are, in and of themselves, insufficient to address all of the security issues associated with Internet voting. Electronic versions of ballots may be subject to Internet-based (or other) attacks that might, for example, delete electronic ballots or otherwise replace or modify electronic election records. With E2E-V systems—as with any voting system—a bad actor could simply claim that his or her vote was not accurately captured. Such claims could eventually be discounted by security experts following the E2E-V trail of evidence. However, with sufficient numbers of bad actors acting simultaneously, confidence in an election outcome could be eroded before all the necessary independent verifications could take place.[24]

---

[22] Ali, Syed Taha and Murray, Judy, "An Overview of End to End Verifiable Voting Systems," in *Real-World Electronic Voting: Design, Analysis and Deployment*, Hao, Feng and Peter Y.A. Ryan, eds. (Boca Raton: CRC Press, 2016).

[23] For one fielded E2E-verification system (Scantegrity) used twice in elections in Takoma Park, MD, the voting process was seen as so much like that experienced previously with optical scan systems that voters did not notice the additional E2E-verifiability mechanisms. With other systems, it is possible that the impact of adding E2E-verification features would be more noticeable.

Scantegrity is paper-based insofar as the casting of ballots. It only uses the Internet as a means through which voters may verify that their votes were included in the tally, or by which anyone can verify that a vote tally is correct, given the posted votes.

[24] Some E2E-verifiable (E2E-V) systems provide mechanisms to address this threat. With the Scantegrity system, for example, voters mark their paper ballots with special pens that reveal a secret code when a voter selects a candidate (the code changes with each ballot). A voter cannot credibly claim to have voted for a candidate without knowing the associated code.

Findings

Complicated and technology-dependent voting systems increase the risk of (and opportunity for) malicious manipulation. Additional methods of review help reduce risks and detect violations of desired security properties.

Conducting rigorous audits enhances confidence in the correctness of election outcomes.

Risk-limiting audits can efficiently establish high confidence in the correctness of election outcomes—even if the equipment used to cast, collect, and tabulate ballots to produce the initial reported outcome is faulty.

States and jurisdictions purchasing election systems should consider in their purchases whether the system has the capacity to match CVRs to physical ballots, as this feature could result in future cost savings when audits are conducted.

While achieving E2E-verfiability, one must still preserve the secret ballot. E2E-V systems generally achieve this by using cryptographic methods to "mask" ballot data while preserving the ability for voters and observers to verify that ballots have been tallied correctly.

E2E-verifiability protocols are not, in and of themselves, sufficient to secure Internet voting, even in theory.

E2E-V election systems enable members of the public to conduct their own audits (or have audits conducted by independent, trusted third parties of their choice).

E2E-V elections can utilize paper ballots or operate purely electronically, the latter offering a means of auditing elections that support voters with visual and/or motor-skill limitations.

Risk-limiting auditing and public auditing using E2E-verifiability may address some security risks associated with tampering. The techniques can be used in combination.

RECOMMENDATIONS

5.5   Each state should require a comprehensive system of post-election audits of processes and outcomes. These audits should be conducted by election officials in a transparent manner, with as much observation by the public as is feasible, up to limits imposed to ensure voter privacy.

5.6   Jurisdictions should conduct audits of voting technology and processes (for voter registration, ballot preparation, voting, election reporting, etc.) after each election. Privacy-protected audit data should be made publicly available to permit others to replicate audit results.

5.7 Audits of election outcomes should include manual examination of statistically appropriate samples of paper ballots cast.

5.8 States should mandate risk-limiting audits prior to the certification of election results. With current technology, this requires the use of paper ballots.[25] States and local jurisdictions should implement risk-limiting audits within a decade. They should begin with pilot programs and work toward full implementation. Risk-limiting audits should be conducted for all federal and state election contests, and for local contests where feasible.

5.9 State and local jurisdictions purchasing election systems should ensure that the systems will support cost-effective risk-limiting audits.

5.10 State and local jurisdictions should conduct and assess pilots of end-to-end-verifiable election systems in elections using paper ballots.

INTERNET VOTING

Overview and Analysis

As more aspects of people's lives move online, it is natural to ask whether the future of voting will also be online. Many people are familiar with and comfortable with the Internet as a tool and conduct what might be considered high-risk transactions (e.g., banking, e-commerce, the transmission of medical records, etc.) online. Internet voting has the potential to increase convenience and perhaps increase participation.[26] With Internet voting, all ballots would be marked using software run on a special voting station or on a voter's own smartphone, tablet, laptop, or desktop computer. Completed ballots would then be transmitted electronically to be tabulated. Although Internet voting offers convenience, it introduces new risks with regard to the integrity and confidentiality of votes as well as the potential for cyberattacks that could make it difficult or impossible for voters to cast their ballots within

---

[25] Risk-limiting audits examine individual randomly selected paper ballots until there is sufficient statistical assurance to demonstrate that the chance that an incorrect reported outcome escaping detection and correction is less than a predetermined risk limit.

[26] Katherine Stewart and Jirka Taylor, analysts for the RAND Corporation, recently concluded that "the observed impact of online voting on voting behaviour to date has been varied. In some cases, it has led to an initial increase in voter turnout. But whether this leads to a long-term trend of sustained voter engagement, particularly among younger people, remains unclear." Citing numerous sources, Stewart and Taylor suggest that online voting "may not be the 'silver bullet' in addressing the wider problem of voter disengagement." See https://www.rand.org/blog/2018/03/online-voting-the-solution-to-declining-political-engagement.html?adbid=986626411103379461&adbpl=tw&adbpr=22545453&adbsc=social_20180418_2261001.

the voting period. Furthermore, the casting of a ballot is an anonymous one-time event. This scenario makes it difficult to identify and correct a miscast vote.

Insecure Internet voting is possible now, but the risks currently associated with Internet voting are more significant than the benefits. Secure Internet voting will likely not be feasible in the near future.

Many vendors, however, currently offer Internet voting systems. Private elections (e.g., corporate shareholder elections) are often conducted primarily over the Internet. Some public elections have allowed Internet voting as an option or even used the Internet as the sole medium for casting votes. As discussed on page 68, voting by fax is sometimes allowed for absentee voters, and completed ballots are sometimes accepted as email attachments.

To ensure secure Internet voting, voters must be supplied with suitable digital credentials that allow them to prove their identity when voting online. Such credentials are supplied to all citizens in some nations (e.g., Estonia). These credentials allow individuals to access a variety of government services. Estonia has extended these services to voting.[27] Neither the U.S. federal government nor the states seem likely to supply universal digital credentials in the near future.[28] If voting is the only purpose for which these credentials are used, voters might easily surrender their credentials to others. Simple PINs and passwords are inadequate for secure voting, and standard email is an inappropriate medium for distributing strong credentials or transmitting marked ballots.[29]

---

[27] Digital credentials may be vulnerable to hacking. In 2017, Estonia suspended the use of its identity smartcards in response to the discovery of a wide-ranging security flaw. More than 750,000 ID cards were affected. See, e.g., "Estonia Has Frozen Its Popular E-Residency ID Cards Because of a Massive Security Flaw," *Business Insider*, November 6, 2017, available at: http://www.businessinsider.com/estonia-freeze-e-residency-id-cards-id-theft-2017-11.

[28] The federal government does provide Common Access Cards (CACs). CACs are "'smart card[s]' about the size of a credit card." They are "standard identification for active duty uniformed Service personnel, Selected Reserve, DoD [U.S. Department of Defense] civilian employees, and eligible contractor personnel . . . [and] the principal card used to enable physical access to buildings and controlled spaces, and" provide "access to DoD computer network and systems." See http://www.cac.mil/common-access-card/.

[29] See, e.g., U.S. Vote Foundation, "The Future of Voting: End-to-end Verifiable Internet Voting—Specifications and Feasibility Study," July 2015, p. 112, available at: https://www.usvotefoundation.org/sites/default/files/E2EVIV_full_report.pdf.

Obstacles to Internet Voting

Many concerns must be addressed before secure Internet voting would be feasible.[30]

Malware

The malware threat present whenever software is used is amplified in the case of Internet voting when voters use personal devices. Such devices may be less well tended and protected than the dedicated election equipment maintained by election officials.

Denial-of-service Attacks

While denial-of-service (DoS) is a risk in any voting medium, it is a mainstay of today's Internet. Many vendors provide services that can mitigate, but not eliminate, these attacks. Unfortunately, the mitigations usually require full decryption of all transmitted data, and these services are performed on systems that are shared with numerous third parties.

Related Technologies

Several technologies are directly relevant to Internet voting.

Secure Channel Technologies

Email is an Internet technology. Most email does not utilize the secure channel technologies commonly used for applications such as online banking and shopping. This makes email voting more vulnerable than many other forms of Internet voting.

Most fax transmissions travel, at least in part, over the Internet and therefore should also be regarded as a form of Internet voting with all of the added risks.

Blockchains

Blockchains are a technology meant to achieve an unalterable, decentralized, public, append-only log of transactions, without any single authority in a position to change the log. In an election context, the "transactions" would be the casting of ballots. A blockchain could therefore act as a virtual electronic ballot box. Blockchains may be managed publicly or by a

---

[30] In addition to the concerns described below, server-side break-ins (demonstrated against the Washington, DC, system in 2010), man-in-the-middle attacks (demonstrated against New South Wales in 2015), and authentication technology vulnerabilities (discovered in Estonia's system in 2017) represent other obstacles that must be addressed before Internet voting would be feasible.

restricted set of managers.[31] Several companies provide, or are attempting to build, voting systems around blockchains.[32]

While the notion of using a blockchain as an immutable ballot box may seem promising, blockchain technology does little to solve the fundamental security issues of elections, and indeed, blockchains introduce additional security vulnerabilities. In particular, if malware on a voter's device alters a vote before it ever reaches a blockchain, the immutability of the block-chain fails to provide the desired integrity, and the voter may never know of the alteration.

Blockchains are decentralized, but elections are inherently centralized. Although blockchains can be effective for decentralized applications, public elections are inherently centralized—requiring election administrators define the contents of ballots, identify the list of eligible voters, and establish the duration of voting. They are responsible for resolving balloting issues, managing vote tabulation, and announcing results. Secure voting requires that these operations be performed verifiably, not that they be performed in a decentralized manner.

While it is true that blockchains offer observability and immutability, in a centralized election scenario, observability and immutability may be achieved more simply by other means. Election officials need only, for example, post digitally signed versions of relevant election-related reports for public observation and download.

Ballots stored on a blockchain are electronic. While paper ballots are directly verifiable by voters, electronic ballots (i.e., ballots on a blockchain) can be more difficult to verify. Software is required to examine postings on blockchain. If such software is corrupted, then verifiability may be illusory. Software independence is not, therefore, achieved through posting ballots on a blockchain: as ballots are represented electronically, software independence may be more difficult to achieve.

The blockchain abstraction, once implemented, provides added points of attack for malicious actors. For example, blockchain "miners" or "stakeholders" (those who add items to the blockchain) have discretionary control over what items are added. Miners/stakeholders might collude to suppress votes from certain populations or regions. Furthermore, blockchain protocols generally yield results that are a consensus of the miners/stakeholders. This consensus may not represent the consensus of the voting public. Miners/stakeholders with sufficient power might also cause confusion and uncertainty about the state of a blockchain by raising doubts about whether a consensus has been reached.

---

[31] Blockchains managed by a restricted set of managers are referred to as *provisioned blockchains*.

[32] Voatz, Inc. and Votem are two such companies.

Blockchains do not provide the anonymity often ascribed to them.[33] In the particular context of elections, voters need to be authorized as eligible to vote and as not having cast more than one ballot in the particular election. Blockchains do not offer means for providing the necessary authorization.

Blockchains do not provide ballot secrecy. If a blockchain is used, then cast ballots must be encrypted or otherwise anonymized to prevent coercion andvote-selling. While E2E-V voting methods may provide the necessary cryptographic tools for this, ordinary blockchain methods do not.

It may be possible to employ blockchains within an election system by addressing the security issues associated with blockchains through the use of additional mechanisms (such as, for example, those provided by E2E-verifiability), but the credit for addressing such problems would lie with the additional mechanisms, not with the use of blockchains.

End-to-end-verifiable Systems

End-to-end-verifiable (E2E-V) technologies can be used in a variety of voting scenarios.

In its 2015 report, the U.S. Vote Foundation asserted that any possible future Internet voting system should utilize E2E-verification, but the report stated that this should not even be attempted before greater experience has been garnered with E2E-V systems deployed and used within in-person voting scenarios.[34]

E2E-V voting mitigates some of the vulnerabilities in Internet voting. However, advances in prevention of malware and DoS attacks need to be realized before *any* Internet voting should be undertaken in public elections—even if E2E-V.

---

[33] A July 13, 2018 federal indictment of twelve Russian operatives, for instance, describes in detail how the operatives were traced and identified through their use of the cryptocurrency bitcoin and its associated blockchain ledger. Count Ten of the indictment (Conspiracy to Launder Money) details how "the Conspirators" used bitcoin and its blockchain ledger in an attempt to "obscure their identities and their links to Russia and the Russian government" and how their use of bitcoin, despite the "perceived anonymity" of blockchains, was then exploited by investigators to identify the operatives. See *United States of America vs. Viktor Borisovich Netyksho, Boris Alekseyevich Antonov, Dmitriy Sergeyevich Badin, Ivan Sergeyevich Yermakov, Aleksey Viktorovich Lukashev, Sergey Aleksandrovich Morgachev, Nikolay Yuryevich Kozachek, Pavel Vyacheslavovich Yershov, Artem Andreyevich Malyshev, Aleksandr Vladimirovich Osadchuk, Aleksey Aleksandrovich Potemkin, and Anatoliy Sergeyevich Kovalev,* Case 1:18-cr-00215-ABJ (2018), pp. 21-22, available at: https://www.justice.gov/file/1080281.

[34] "The Future of Voting: End-to-end Verifiable Internet Voting—Specifications and Feasibility Study," p. v.

Findings

All Internet voting schemes (including those that are E2E-V) are vulnerable to DoS attacks.

The Internet is not currently a suitable medium for the transmission of marked ballots, as Internet-based voting systems in which votes are cast on remote computers or other electronic devices and submitted electronically cannot be made adequately secure today.

E2E-verifiability may mitigate many of the threats associated with Internet voting.

Conducting secure and credible Internet elections will require substantial scientific advances.

The use of blockchains in an election scenario would do little to address the major security requirements of voting, such as voter verifiability. The security contributions offered by blockchains are better obtained by other means. In the particular case of Internet voting, blockchain methods do not redress the security issues associated with Internet voting.

RECOMMENDATIONS

5.11 **At the present time, the Internet (or any network connected to the Internet) should not be used for the return of marked ballots.**[35,36] **Further, Internet voting should not be used in the future until and unless very robust guarantees of security and verifiability are developed and in place, as no known technology guarantees the secrecy, security, and verifiability of a marked ballot transmitted over the Internet.**[37]

5.12 **U.S. Election Assistance Commission standards and state laws should be revised to support pilot programs to explore and validate new election technologies and practices. Election officials are encouraged to seek expert and public comment on proposed new election technology before it is piloted.**

---

[35] Inclusive of transmission via email or fax or via phone lines.

[36] The Internet is an acceptable medium for the transmission of unmarked ballots to voters so long as voter privacy is maintained and the integrity of the received ballot is protected.

[37] If secure Internet voting becomes feasible and is adopted, alternative ballot-casting options should be made available to those individuals who do not have sufficient access to the Internet.

6

Analysis of Systemic Issues

In this chapter, the committee discusses election administrator and poll worker training, the voting technology marketplace, and the federal role in elections.

ELECTION ADMINISTRATOR AND POLL WORKER TRAINING

Overview and Analysis

Proper training of election administrators is a key component in ensuring well-run elections and in the mitigation of disruptions in the voting process.

Voting jurisdictions in the United States come in many sizes. Fully one-third are small towns with small budgets, part-time and volunteer staff, and limited access to information technology (IT) expertise. Between and during elections, staff generally have other responsibilities (e.g., recording deeds, issuing licenses, etc.). In most locations, poll workers have minimal training. They work intermittently during election cycles, often only on Election Day.

In larger jurisdictions, election administrators supervise larger staffs who may have attended some continuing education classes on election management offered by other in-state organizations of local public officials or the state election authority. In-service groups such as The Election Center,[1] along with national organizations of public officials, offer profes-

---

[1] See https://www.electioncenter.org/.

sional certificate programs in election administration. Auburn University, the University of Minnesota, and Kennesaw State University (Georgia) offer undergraduate and graduate courses in election management.[2] Courses include an introduction to the election process, election design, data analysis, voter participation, and strategic management. Courses in cybersecurity are beginning to be offered. Although some jurisdictions (e.g., Los Angeles County and New York State) now require training certification for election workers, there are no national accrediting standards for an election management curriculum at universities or community colleges.

Modern elections are more complex and consequently require election administrators with more specialized skills. Training and education programs in election administration are limited, and there are scant resources available to professionalize the election workforce. Many election administrators receive only minimal professional education and training beyond on-the-job experience. Increasing technical and management challenges require staff with more advanced qualifications and training, and it may be necessary to bring skilled people from other disciplines (including but not limited to IT and cybersecurity) into election administration. This reality may necessitate a review of hiring practices by election administrators.

Because most election administrators have other responsibilities, time and access to education and training opportunities are limited. Tight municipal and county budgets compound these constraints. Cross-institutional cooperation may provide a means of lowering barriers to better training and education in those communities with limited resources.

State and local election administrators are highly dependent on system vendors to install and maintain election systems, and they do not have access to the most comprehensive and current resources for implementing, checking, and making enhancements to the IT supporting their election systems.

Findings

There is a need to develop the professional election workforce in ways that enable it to handle new challenges in election administration.

There are growing gaps in election administrators' information technology skills, in their ability to access skilled IT professionals, and in their ability to detect, prevent, and respond to cyberattacks.

---

[2] Hale, Katherine, Auburn University, presentation to the committee, December 8, 2017, Denver, CO.

Further, the Network of Schools of Public Policy, Affairs, and Administration (NASPAA) is establishing an "Election Commons" through which schools can collaborate on course development and cross-registration in election administration offerings. See http://www.naspaa.org/students/InternshipSum17_ElectionAdministration.pdf.

RECOMMENDATIONS

6.1   Congress should provide adequate funding for the U.S. Election Assistance Commission to continue to serve as a national clearinghouse of information on election administration.

6.2   The U.S. Election Assistance Commission, with assistance from the national associations of state and local election administrators, should encourage, develop, and enhance information technology training programs to educate state and local technical staff on effective election administration.

6.3   Universities and community colleges should increase efforts to design curricula that address the growing organizational management and information technology needs of the election community.

THE VOTING TECHNOLOGY MARKETPLACE

Overview and Analysis

The 2000 presidential election was the impetus for a national transition from mechanical to electronic voting machines and from manual to automated processes. The election thrust the shortcomings of punch card voting technology into the spotlight and exposed a need for more reliable voting systems. As part of the 2002 Help America Vote Act (HAVA), Congress authorized the allocation of $3 billion to the states, primarily for the purchasing of new voting technology.[3] HAVA also created the U.S. Election Assistance Commission (EAC), an independent entity that would "serve as a national clearinghouse and resource for the compilation of information and review of procedures with respect to the administration of Federal elections"[4] and develop "voluntary voting system guidelines."[5] The EAC was responsible for administering HAVA funds.

The infusion of HAVA funding led to the development and deployment of new voting machines, and in particular, a more widespread deployment of Direct Recording Electronic (DRE) devices. The EAC reports that, "through September 30, 2015, a total of $3,247,294,645 has been made

---

[3] See HAVA Section 101. In addition to upgrading voting systems, states were to use HAVA funds for the purposes of "improving the administration of elections for Federal office;" "educating voters concerning voting procedures, voting rights, and voting technology;" "training election officials, poll workers, and election volunteers;" and "improving the accessibility and quantity of polling places, including providing physical access for individuals with disabilities, providing nonvisual access for individuals with visual impairments, and providing assistance to Native Americans, Alaska Native citizens, and to individuals with limited proficiency in the English language."

[4] See HAVA, Part 1, Election Assistance Commission.

[5] See HAVA Part 3, Section 221.

available to the 50 States, American Samoa, the District of Columbia, Guam, the Commonwealth of Puerto Rico and the United States Virgin Islands (hereinafter referred to as States) under HAVA" and that "States have reported total expenditures of $3,197,438,400 or 89 percent of total Federal funds and accrued interest available" to them.[6] Looked at another way, "36 of 55 (65 percent) states and territories in the US have less than 10 percent of their originally allocated HAVA funds left (including interest) and another 14 states and territories (25 percent) have less than half of their funding left."[7]

HAVA provided much-needed funding for improved voting technology. However, at the time the Act was passed, available machines had flaws related to both security and operational aspects. For instance, DRE machines did not produce a means for voter verification and did not adequately address the needs of the disabled community. Furthermore, HAVA provided only a one-time infusion of funds. There were no provisions to provide funding for the replacement of voting machines in the future, and to satisfy statutory requirements, many states made significant equipment purchases at the onset of funding. The conduct of elections is, however, an ongoing (and evolving process) and periodic infusions of funding do not allow for a consistent program of improvements.

"The depletion of the HAVA funds has significant implications today, as the systems deployed as a result of HAVA are nearing the end of their useful life and need to be replaced. The service life of most new voting hardware and software purchased and installed immediately after the passing of HAVA is 10-15 years, and states now lacking HAVA funds have to go to extraordinary lengths to keep their aging systems operational."[8]

"The election technology industry has come to be characterized by a consolidated, highly concentrated market dominated by a few major vendors, where industry growth and competition are constrained." "The firms in the election technology industry sell integrated voting solutions, typically including a package of hardware, software, services and support. The industry has a two-tier structure with . . . Election Systems and Software ("ES&S"), Hart Intercivic ("Hart") and Dominion Voting Systems," the largest vendors, in the top tier.[9] In the second tier, a few small firms provide

---

[6] U.S. Election Assistance Commission, "Annual Grant Expenditure Report, Fiscal Year 2015," p. 2, available at: https://www.eac.gov/assets/1/28/Final%20FY%202015%20Grants%20Report.pdf.

[7] See University of Pennsylvania, Wharton School Public Policy Initiative, "The Business of Voting: Market Structure and Innovation in the Election Technology Industry," 2016, p. 12, available at: https://publicpolicy.wharton.upenn.edu/live/files/270-the-business-of-voting.

[8] Ibid, p. 13.

[9] Ibid, pp. 14-15. From this tier, the committee received testimony from Hart InterCivic. ES&S and Dominion Voting Systems declined to make presentations to the committee.

specialized technology (e.g., for the disabled) or serve small markets.[10] The largest voting technology vendor, ES&S, has about 460 employees. The customer base for voting machines is fragmented, and purchasers have widely varying levels of technological and purchasing expertise. Furthermore, buying power is limited for all but the largest customers.

The price of voting machines is usually not made public, and costs vary depending on factors such as the number of units purchased, the vendor chosen, and whether or not maintenance agreements are also purchased. The National Conference of State Legislatures (NCLS) estimates that the cost of a DRE voting machine ranges from $2,500 to $3,000 per unit, exclusive of peripherals such as voter-verified paper audit trail (VVPAT) and accessibility features. NCLS estimates that the cost per unit for precinct optical scanners ranges from $2,500 to $5,000 and that the cost of a central count optical scanner ranges from $70,000 to $100,000.[11] "The Brennan Center estimates it could cost well over $1 billion to replace all of the voting machines that should be replaced in the next few years."[12]

Some election administrators are exploring alternatives to the current private-sector, for-profit marketplace for election systems. Several jurisdictions are exploring the development of open-source or publicly-owned voting systems that use commercial off-the shelf (COTS) hardware in an effort to reduce both the initial cost and ongoing software maintenance costs associated with proprietary systems.

The usual model of open-source software is that with a license, a user has access to the source code and can read, use, or modify it in accordance with the license.[13] Widely used open source software is normally maintained by an organization that provides documentation and distribution sites. Any software developer can propose software changes and modifications, which are vetted by one or more experts, who integrate the changes into the distributed software. Hence the organization creates a kind of standardization, for users whose individual modifications are limited. The transparency provided by the availability of source code increases confidence that the software functions as intended. The participation of the user community aids software quality (since problems are publicly identified and

---

[10] From this tier, the committee received testimony from Everyone Counts, the Five Cedars Group, Free & Fair, and Democracy Live.

[11] National Conference of State Legislatures, "Voting Equipment," available at: http://www.ncsl.org/research/elections-and-campaigns/voting-equipment.aspx.

[12] Norden, Lawrence and Christopher Famighetti, Brennan Center for Justice, *America's Voting Machines at Risk*, 2015, p. 17, available at: https://www.brennancenter.org/sites/default/files/publications/Americas_Voting_Machines_At_Risk.pdf.

[13] Most license agreements specify that users maintain the openness of the software they acquire, provide acknowledgement of use in a product, and respect the licenses of components that come from other organizations; some require that modifications also be shared.

corrected) and continuously improves the software base. Since the software itself has only nominal cost, revenue comes from providing support and enhancements. The cost of entry to the provider market is low, enabling competition that tends to drive down costs.[14]

Since 2005, for instance, the Travis County (TX) Clerk has been studying how to improve the security and efficiency of electronic voting systems while making incremental changes in existing processes to anticipate and effectively confront emerging threats. Travis County collaborated with experts in computer science, cryptography and computer security, statistics, and human factor engineering to build a voting system to resolve concerns about electronic voting. That system, STAR Vote (Secure, Transparent, Auditable, Reliable), was designed to offer the speed and accuracy of electronic voting as well as advantages for voters with disabilities. It also provided a paper ballot selection summary for recount and audit purposes.

STAR Vote offered end-to-end-verifiable (E2E-V) elections and included support for risk-limiting audits with enhanced voter privacy. The system would have offered two paper record proofs. One provided a record of a voter's selections. This was deposited into a ballot box at the polling place. The precinct ballot counter matched an electronic copy of the marked ballot stored in the ballot-marking device to the paper record inserted into the ballot box. Ballots with stray marks or those that did not match the electronic version of the ballot were rejected. The second paper record was a receipt with a hash code that the voter retained. Following an election, the voter could access an online bulletin board to verify that the code printed on his or her receipt was included in a list of codes representing all ballots tallied.

A Request for Proposals (RFP) seeking entities to build STAR Vote was issued in late 2016, and proposals were submitted by prospective vendors early in 2017. However, the proposals received were not sufficient to build a complete voting system, and Travis County was unable to pursue the building of STAR Vote.[15]

In 2009, the Los Angeles (LA) County Registrar-Recorder/County Clerk launched the Voting System Assessment Project (VSAP) project when it determined that no system on the market was adequate to meet the needs of the electorate in LA County (the project was later renamed Voting Solutions for All People, as it changed focus from assessment to implementation). The project is working to design and launch a new voting system for the county. The goals of VSAP are to implement publicly owned voting sys-

---

[14] While the cost of entry to the provider market is low, open-source systems need to be maintained, and this maintenance is typically provided by vendors at a cost.

[15] DeBeauvior, Dana, "STAR Vote – A Change of Plans," September 26, 2017, available at: www.traviscountyelections.org. Ms. DeBeauvoir is a member of the committee that authored the current report.

tems; spur innovation in the voting system market; encourage a regulatory environment that allows for the development, certification, and implementation of publicly owned, voter-centered systems; establish LA County as a new model for voting system development and implementation; and make research findings available for other jurisdictions to utilize and replicate the LA County design process where desired.[16] Currently, VSAP is developing a vote tally system, conducting a vote center placement assessment, and soliciting for system manufacturing and certification.[17]

Prime III is voting software developed at Auburn University in 2003 through a public-private partnership.[18] The system was designed to be "a secure, multimodal electronic voting system that delivers the necessary system security, integrity and user satisfaction safeguards in a user-friendly interface that accommodates all people regardless of ability."[19] Currently, Prime III is the only open-source voting system that has been used in state, federal, and local elections. In 2015, New Hampshire adopted Prime III and renamed it One4All. The One4All system was used in 2016 primaries as well as the presidential election.[20]

In the voting marketplace, the STAR vote proposal, the VSAP project, and the Prime III system are all possible bases for an open-source software base. In this setting, jurisdictions, singly or collectively, would have to assume the costs and time associated with the certification of their open-source voting system.[21]

Public-private partnerships could spark innovation in the voting technology marketplace. Creating a partnership with academia might generate innovations in the voting technology marketplace. The ES&S ExpressVote

---

[16] Bennett, Kenneth and Monica Flores, County of Los Angeles County (CA) Registrar-Recorder/County Clerk, presentation to the committee, December 7, 2017, Denver, CO.

[17] Circa December 2017. LA County has since indicated that the system will run on an open-source platform as opposed to open-source software. In June 2018, a contract was awarded to Smartmatic to assist the county with the development, manufacturing, and implementation of the system.

[18] The partnership included the National Science Foundation, the U.S. Election Assistance Commission, Auburn University, Clemson University, and the University of Florida. Dr. Juan E. Gilbert, who serves as a member of the committee that authored the current report, was a developer of Prime III.

[19] See http://www.primevotingsystem.com/.

[20] New Hampshire Assistant Secretary of State Tom Manning stated, "The old system required us to pay a little bit less than $250,000 a year in licensing fees for the software that ran in [sic] and then the telephone lines that we needed to connect to our data center would run us about $10,000 a month." See Ganley, Rick and Michael Brindley, "Tablet-Based Ballot System for Blind Voters to Debut During N.H. Primary," New Hampshire Public Radio, February 8, 2016, available at: http://nhpr.org/post/tablet-based-ballot-system-blind-voters-debut-during-nh-primary#stream/0.

[21] See "The Business of Voting: Market Structure and Innovation in the Election Technology Industry," pp. 32-33.

Universal Voting System is an example of a product that resulted from a public-private partnership between ES&S and the Prime III team of academic researchers.

Developing open interfaces between systems can provide opportunities for component-based systems where the components are from different suppliers, and Common Data Formats (CDFs) have been developed to facilitate interoperability. Electronic products used by election officials must be able to share data between devices (or with a common host) if they are to be part of an integrated election administration process. As the "data language" used by such products tends to be proprietary, devices from one manufacturer might not be able to communicate with products from another manufacturer. Election officials may, therefore, need to purchase all their election systems from a single vendor.[22]

The National Institute of Standards and Technology is currently developing a CDF for election systems.[23]

Findings

There is a lack of dedicated funding for new voting systems. Elections funding competes with other state and local programs, and election funding may not receive high priority.

The high cost of maintenance agreements and the bundling of system hardware, software, and services limits election administrators' flexibility with regard to future purchases of voting systems. The expense of purchasing electronic voting systems or purchasing enough extra inventory of paper, optical scan ballots (and resources to secure them) to satisfy the needs of vote centers or early voting programs is not affordable for many local jurisdictions.

Great strides have been made to reform the voting system certification process. Compliance is voluntary and standard setting is difficult, but the efforts of the U.S. Election Assistance Commission and the National Institute of Standards and Technology should be applauded.

A standard national certification process would help to increase competition among voting technology vendors.

The relatively small and underfunded market for voting technology presents an obstacle for new entrants and may inhibit the use of the latest devices in election administration.

---

[22] National Institute of Standards and Technology, "An Introduction to the Common Data Format Project," available at: https://collaborate.nist.gov/voting/bin/view/Voting/WhyIsACDFNeeded.

[23] See National Institute of Standards and Technology, "The NIST Interoperability Public Working Group and Common Data Format (CDF) for Election Systems Project," available at: https://www.nist.gov/itl/voting/interoperability.

The structure of the current election technology marketplace provides limited incentives for technological innovation.

There are alternatives to the current private-sector, for-profit marketplace for election systems.

RECOMMENDATIONS

6.4   Congress should:
   a. create incentive programs for public-private partnerships to develop modern election technology;
   b. appropriate funds for distribution by the U.S. Election Assistance Commission for the ongoing modernization of election systems; and
   c. authorize and appropriate funds to the National Institute of Standards and Technology to establish Common Data Formats for auditing, voter registration, and other election systems.

6.5   Along with Congress, states should allocate funds for the modernization of election systems.

6.6   The U.S. Election Assistance Commission and the National Institute of Standards and Technology should continue to collaborate on changes to the certification process that encourage the modernization of voting systems.

6.7   The National Institute of Standards and Technology should complete the Common Data Format standard for election systems.

6.8   New election systems should conform to the Common Data Format standard developed by the National Institute of Standards and Technology.

THE FEDERAL ROLE

Overview and Analysis

As noted in previous chapters, elections in the United States are administered in a decentralized fashion. States and local jurisdictions carry out the primary functions and processes associated with federal and state elections. States and local jurisdictions, consequently, assume responsibility for the majority of expenses associated with election administration.

The federal government has, however, a legitimate role to play in election administration. The U.S. Constitution gives the federal government ample authority to regulate elections, and over the past 50 years, Congress has exercised federal authority in many contexts. The Elections Clause (Article I, Section 4, Clause 1) of the Constitution specifies that the states will determine the "Times, Places, and Manner" of congressional elections, and allows Congress to "make or alter" states' regulations. Moreover, each amendment to the Constitution that prevents discrimination in voting rights—the 15th Amendment (race), the 19th Amendment (sex), the 24th Amendment (poll taxes), the 26th Amendment (age)—grants Congress the power "to enforce this article by appropriate legislation." Likewise, the 14th Amendment, which the Supreme Court has interpreted to provide protection for voting rights even for groups beyond those specifically enumerated by those other amendments and to protect against other undue burdens on the right to vote, contains similar enforcement provisions.

Congress has exercised its constitutional authority to regulate elections in a range of contexts. One of the earliest pieces of election-related legislation was passed by Congress in 1842. It required that each representative be elected by a separate district. [24] Soon after, in 1845, Congress chose a single date for all national elections—the first Tuesday after the first Monday in November.[25] As discussed in Chapter 4 (see pp. 55-56), Congress has used its authority to regulate the mechanics of elections ever since.

The federal role in elections has increased over time in response to issues of national concern. With each effort for greater national uniformity in elections or federal voting rights protection, concerns about localism and state sovereignty are raised. Elections continue to be administered by states and localities, often against a backdrop of federal regulations that ensure protection of voting rights. Nevertheless, great variation exists among states in certain basic components of the electoral process. This diversity is a double-edged sword. On the one hand, the quality of election administration can vary based on where a voter lives. On the other, the lack of a single national voting system may offer some protection against widespread compromise of the results of an election. That limited protection may be negated, however, when attackers can use comprehensive data analysis to target voting jurisdictions that can change the outcome of an election.[26]

When exercising federal authority, the government has recognized that, while election administration is primarily a state and local responsibility, there are occasions where the federal government should play a leading role by providing resources that will nudge election administrators in certain

---

[24] The Act, the Apportionment Act of 1842, states that, "in every case where a State is entitled to more than one Representative, the number to which each State shall be entitled under this apportionment shall be elected by districts, composed of contiguous territory, equal in number to the number of Representatives to which said State may be entitled; no one district electing more than one Representative."

[25] Prior to this time, Congress allowed states to conduct presidential elections at any point in the 34 days before the first Wednesday in December—the meeting of the state electoral colleges.

[26] Potential attackers could use such data to target those jurisdictions that are deemed easiest to compromise.

directions (e.g., to upgrade election technology) or that will provide access to intelligence information pertinent to national security.

The federal government also has a role to play in ensuring the resilience of the nation in the face of cyberattacks. As noted throughout this report, protecting America's election infrastructure became a national security concern in the wake of Russian cyber efforts to target U.S. voting databases and systems. These efforts prompted the federal government, through the U.S. Department of Homeland Security (DHS), to designate election infrastructure as a subsector of the existing Government Facilities critical infrastructure sector, placing it on par with sectors such as banking and electricity. This designation prioritized for the first time the protection of election systems as a national security issue, identified DHS as the lead federal agency to coordinate with state and local officials, and provided states with access to government national security information.

The critical infrastructure designation was met with resistance in the elections community. Immediately after the nation's election systems were given critical infrastructure status, the National Association of Secretaries of State (NASS) issued a statement wherein it asserted that

> No credible evidence of hacking, including attempted hacking of voting machines or vote counting, was ever presented or discovered in any state. State and local autonomy over elections is our greatest asset against malicious cyberattacks and manipulation. Our decentralized, low-connectivity electoral process is inherently designed to withstand such threats.

"While we recognize," the statement continued, "the need to share information on threats and risk mitigation in our elections at all levels of government, as we did throughout the 2016 cycle, it is unclear why a critical infrastructure classification is now necessary for this purpose."[27] NASS provides further clarification on its website:

> While NASS members recognize the need to share information on threats and risk mitigation in our elections at all levels of government, Secretaries of State oppose the critical infrastructure designation based on the federal government's continued lack of transparency and clarity with chief state election officials on plans for implementing the designation.[28]

However, the critical infrastructure designation only allows DHS to provide support to "the private sector and state, local, tribal, and territorial

---

[27] National Association of Secretaries of State, "NASS Statement on Critical Infrastructure Designation for Elections," January 9, 2017, available at: https://www.nass.org/node/228.

[28] National Association of Secretaries of State, "Elections as Critical Infrastructure: What Does It Mean?," available at: https://www.nass.org/initiatives/election-cybersecurity.

governments in the management of their cyber risk" and "provide technical assistance in the event of a cyber incident, as requested." The department can provide (1) "automated, recurring scans of Internet facing systems that provide the perspective of the vulnerabilities and configuration errors that a potential adversary could see;" (2) "penetration testing, social engineering, wireless access discovery, database scanning, and operating system scanning;" (3) "alerts, analysis reports, bulletins, best practices, cyber threat indicators, guidance, points-of-contact, security tips, and technical documents to stakeholders;" (4) "regionally located personnel who engage state and local governments, election crime coordinators, and vendors to offer immediate and sustained assistance, coordination, and outreach to prepare and protect from cyber and physical threats;" and (5) access to "cybersecurity operations centers that maintain close coordination among the private sector, government officials, the intelligence community, and law enforcement to provide situational awareness and incident response, as appropriate."[29]

As discussed in Chapter 1, Congress created the EAC to serve as a clearinghouse for election administration research and information and to award federal funds to allow states to replace antiquated voting systems and to improve election administration. A full commission has four members, and currently there are two vacancies. Importantly, any action of the Commission authorized by HAVA requires approval of at least three of its members. Federal funding for the EAC is currently less than $10 million/year and includes funds for transfer to the National Institute of Standards and Technology for election reform administration activities.

Although there are strong efforts by research groups and nonprofit organizations to gather data to inform election-related decisions and legislation, additional work is needed. The federal government has a role in sponsoring (1) research that distinguishes beliefs about election issues from evidence-based understanding; and (2) pilot programs to explore novel solutions to problems identified in Chapters 4 and 5. Broad statistics on voting patterns, the effect of by-mail voting, the effect of various factors on voter turnout, and other questions need to be refined to reflect particular regions and socioeconomic factors. The influence of technological advances such as machine learning and data mining on the elections system needs to be better understood. Though the conduct of elections is largely delegated to the states, the federal government has a responsibility to sponsor research that protects the integrity of elections.

---

[29] Hale, Geoffrey, U.S. Department of Homeland Security, presentation to the committee (Slides 4 and 7), April 4, 2017, Washington, DC, available at: http://sites.nationalacademies.org/cs/groups/pgasite/documents/webpage/pga_178365.pdf.

Findings

There is no centralized election body that establishes rules for national elections or reports the results of national elections.

The decentralized character of U.S. election administration provides a check against a widespread technological breakdown or cyberattack. At the same time, it increases the number of potential vectors of attack against election administration, many of which are small jurisdictions that are under-resourced to respond adequately to modern cyber-risks.

The range and heterogeneity of local statutes and election administration challenges prevent implementation of a single uniform voting system across the country.

There is no central location wherein problems (e.g., long lines, malfunctioning machines, etc.) arising on Election Day are reported, compiled, and analyzed.

The federal government has increased its involvement in the administration of national elections in response to serious system concerns.

While funds allocated under HAVA were critical to the improvement of elections, without sustained federal funding, jurisdictions may be unable to purchase equipment that is easy to use, accessible, secure, and reliable.

The nature of threats to election systems is changing as state and non-state actors attempt to undermine election systems through cyber and information warfare.

Addressing foreign government assaults on election databases and systems require new approaches and better federal-state collaboration. States and local governments do not have an independent ability to protect election infrastructure against nation-state attacks.

The designation by DHS of election systems as a subsector of the existing government facilities critical infrastructure sector is correct and appropriate. This designation reflects appropriately the need for sophisticated technical expertise and sharing of intelligence information required to protect the nation's election infrastructure.

The EAC has a vital role to play in improving election administration.

The federal government has an important role to play in understanding the impact of technological changes on the conduct of elections and in evaluating possible remedies to election threats.

RECOMMENDATION

6.9   To improve the overall performance of the election process:
   a. The president should nominate and Congress should confirm a full U.S. Election Assistance Commission and ensure that the U.S. Election Assistance Commission has sufficient members to sustain a quorum.

b. Congress should fully fund the U.S. Election Assistance Commission to carry out its existing functions.

c. Congress should require state and local election officials to provide the U.S. Election Assistance Commission with data on voting system failures during elections as well as information on other difficulties arising during elections (e.g., long lines, fraudulent voting, intrusions into voter registration databases, etc.). This information should be publicly available.

7

Securing the Future of Voting

As this report illustrates, voting in the United States is a complicated process that involves multiple levels of government, personnel with a variety of skills and capabilities, and numerous electronic systems that interact in the performance of a multitude of tasks. Unfortunately, our current system is vulnerable to internal and external threats.

As the U.S. elections system has undergone significant technological changes and adapted to meet changing needs, the American electorate has largely remained confident that the ballots it casts are accurately counted and tabulated. Nevertheless, recent events make it clear that our system of voting must evolve in order to also protect against external actors who wish to undermine confidence in democratic institutions. The new foreign threat has profound implications for the future of voting and obliges us to seriously reexamine both the conduct of elections in the United States and the role of federal and state governments in securing our elections. We must think strategically and creatively about the administration of U.S. elections. We must confront barriers (both real and perceived) that inhibit partnerships that would facilitate reliable, accessible, verifiable, and secure voting. We must foster an environment that promotes innovation in election systems technology, provides election administrators with human resource tools to increase the professionalization of the election workforce, allocates appropriate resources for the operation of elections, and better secures elections by developing auditing tools that provide assurances that ballots cast are counted and tabulated correctly and that the results of elections are accurate.

We have witnessed tremendous technological advances in recent decades, but we must give careful consideration to the adoption of technologies that might increase convenience for voters. We do not, at present, have the technology to offer a secure method to support Internet voting. It is certainly possible that individuals will be able to vote via the Internet in the future, but technical concerns preclude the possibility of doing so securely at present. It is difficult to secure the electronic systems used in voting even now. In systems ranging from electronic voter registration databases and electronic pollbooks to voting systems, corresponding physical records are essential for matching purposes. Furthermore, election administrators must have the capacity to conduct routine audits on their electronic systems throughout the election process.

To fully address the challenges inherent in electronic election systems and to prevent foreign interference, federal, state, and local officials must adopt innovative measures to ensure that the results of elections reflect the will of the electorate. Election systems in the future must be not only secure but also adaptive and resilient. To ensure the integrity of the voting process, we must be constantly vigilant, have the ability to verify and safeguard data, make continuous improvements in voting processes and technologies, and, through engagement and transparency, consistently educate and reassure our electorate. If the challenges currently facing our election systems are ignored, we risk an erosion of confidence in our elections system and in the integrity of our election processes.

THE ROLE OF THE U.S. ELECTION ASSISTANCE COMMISSION AND FEDERAL AGENCIES

The U.S. Election Assistance Commission (EAC) performs an important role in U.S. elections by serving as a clearinghouse for information on election administration, establishing voting system guidelines, accrediting testing laboratories, certifying voting systems, and overseeing the disbursement of funds for the improvement of elections. Each of these functions enhances the conduct of elections. To perform these functions properly, the EAC depends on adequate funding and resources.

The National Institute of Standards and Technology (NIST) assists the EAC by providing critical technical expertise. Working together, NIST and the EAC have made numerous contributions to the improvement of electronic voting systems. However, as this report indicates, there are many technical obstacles to overcome if electronic voting systems are to be secured from external and internal threats.

Other federal agencies, such as the National Science Foundation and the U.S. Department of Defense, have, through their research programs, made positive contributions to our understanding of elections and election administration.

RECOMMENDATIONS

7.1 Congress should provide appropriate funding to the U.S. Election Assistance Commission to carry out the functions assigned to it in the Help America Vote Act of 2002 as well as those articulated in this report.

7.2 Congress should authorize and provide appropriate funding to the National Institute of Standards and Technology to carry out its current elections-related functions and to perform the additional functions articulated in this report.

7.3 Congress should authorize and fund immediately a major initiative on voting that supports basic, applied, and translational research relevant to the administration, conduct, and performance of elections. This initiative should include academic centers to foster collaboration both across disciplines and with state and local election officials and industry.

The U.S. Election Assistance Commission, National Institute of Standards and Technology, U.S. Department of Homeland Security, National Science Foundation, and U.S. Department of Defense should sponsor research to:

- determine means for providing voters with the ability to easily check whether a ballot sent by mail has been dispatched to him or her and, subsequently, whether his or her marked ballot has been received and accepted by the appropriate elections officials;
- evaluate the reliability of various approaches (e.g., signature, biometric, etc.) to voter authentication;
- explore options for testing the usability and comprehensibility of ballot designs created within tight, pre-election timeframes;
- understand the effects of coercion, vote buying, theft, etc., especially among disadvantaged groups, on voting by mail and to devise technologies for reducing this threat;
- determine voter practices regarding the verification of ballot marking device–generated ballots and the likelihood of voters, both with and without disabilities, will recognize errors or omissions;
- assess the potential benefits and risks of Internet voting;
- evaluate end-to-end-verifiable election systems in various election scenarios and assess the potential utility of such systems for Internet voting; and
- address any other issues that arise concerning the integrity of U.S. elections.

CONCLUSION

As a nation, we have the capacity to build an elections system for the future, but doing so requires focused attention from citizens, federal, state, and local governments, election administrators, and innovators in academia and industry. It also requires a commitment of appropriate resources. Representative democracy only works if all eligible citizens can participate in elections, have their ballots accurately cast, counted, and tabulated, and be confident that their ballots have been accurately cast, counted, and tabulated.

Appendixes

Appendix A

Biographical Information of Committee and Staff

CO-CHAIRS

LEE C. BOLLINGER has served as the president of Columbia University since 2002 and is the longest serving Ivy League president. He is Columbia's first Seth Low Professor of the University, a member of the Columbia Law School faculty, and one of the country's foremost First Amendment scholars. His book, *The Free Speech Century*, co-edited with Geoffrey R. Stone, will be published in the fall of 2018 by Oxford University Press.

From 1996 to 2002, Bollinger was the president of the University of Michigan at Ann Arbor. He led the school's litigation in *Grutter v. Bollinger* and *Gratz v. Bollinger*, resulting in Supreme Court decisions that upheld and clarified the importance of diversity as a compelling justification for affirmative action in higher education. He speaks and writes frequently about the value of racial, cultural, and socio-economic diversity to American society through opinion columns, media interviews, and public appearances.

Bollinger received his Juris Doctor from Columbia Law School. He served as a law clerk to Judge Wilfred Feinberg of the United States Court of Appeals for the Second Circuit and Chief Justice Warren Burger of the Supreme Court. Bollinger went on to join the faculty of the University of Michigan Law School in 1973, becoming dean of the school in 1987. He became provost of Dartmouth College in 1994 before returning to the University of Michigan in 1996 as president.

MICHAEL A. McROBBIE is the 18th president of Indiana University (IU). Dr. McRobbie joined IU in 1997 as vice president for information technology and chief information officer, and was appointed vice president for research in 2003. He was named interim provost and vice president for academic affairs for Indiana University's Bloomington campus in 2006 and became president the following year. He is now one of the longest serving public university presidents in the Association of American Universities.

As president, McRobbie has led the largest ever academic restructuring and expansion of IU, with the establishment of 10 new schools, over $2.5 billion of new construction, and the establishment of the university's Global Gateway Network of offices around the world.

As chief information officer, McRobbie was responsible for a number of initiatives of national importance, including the establishment of the Global Network Operations Center, now responsible for the operation and management of over 20 national and international research and education networks including the Internet2 network, the National Oceanic and Atmospheric Administration's research network, and international connections to major research and education networks in the Asia-Pacific, Europe and Africa, and the establishment of the Research and Education Network Information Sharing and Analysis Center (REN-ISAC) focused on network based cybersecurity issues for its 540 national and international members —the only ISAC in higher education.

McRobbie holds faculty appointments in computer science, philosophy, and cognitive science and informatics and has been an active researcher in information technology and logic over the course of his career. He is a fellow of the American Academy of Arts and Sciences, an honorary fellow of the Australian Academy of Humanities and a member of the Council on Foreign Relations. He was awarded the Sagamore of the Wabash by the governor of Indiana in 2007 and 2017. McRobbie's commitment to international engagement in higher education has been recognized through the receipt of the International Citizen of the Year award in Indiana and five honorary degrees from foreign universities. A native of Australia, in 2010 he was made an Officer of the Order of Australia, Australia's national honors system.

MEMBERS

ANDREW W. APPEL is the Eugene Higgins Professor of Computer Science at Princeton University, where he has been on the faculty since 1986. He served as department chair from 2009 to 2015. His research is in software verification, computer security, programming languages and compilers, and technology policy. He received his A.B. summa cum laude in physics from Princeton in 1981 and his Ph.D. in computer science from Carnegie

Mellon University in 1985. He has been editor-in-chief of *ACM Transactions on Programming Languages and Systems* and is a fellow of the ACM (Association for Computing Machinery). He has worked on fast N-body algorithms (1980s), Standard ML of New Jersey (1990s), Foundational Proof-Carrying Code (2000s), and the Verified Software Toolchain (2010s). He is the author of several scientific papers on voting machines and election technology, served as an expert witness on two voting-related court cases in New Jersey, and has taught a course at Princeton on election machinery.

JOSH BENALOH is senior cryptographer at Microsoft Research and an affiliate faculty member in the University of Washington School of Computer Science and Engineering. He holds an S.B. in mathematics from Massachusetts Institute of Technology and M.S., M. Phil., and Ph.D. degrees in computer science from Yale University where his 1987 doctoral dissertation "Verifiable Secret-Ballot Elections" introduced the use of homomorphic encryption as a paradigm to enable election tallies to be verified by individual voters and observers without having to trust election equipment, vendors, or personnel.

Benaloh served for 17 years as a director of the International Association for Cryptologic Research, and he currently serves on the Coordinating Committee of the Election Verification Network. He has published and spoken extensively on cryptography, policy, and election technologies and is an author of the widely covered 2015 "Keys Under Doormats" report, which explores the technical implications of restrictions on cryptography and has influenced the ongoing political debate. Benaloh is also an author of the 2015 U.S. Vote Foundation report on the viability of end-to-end-verifiable Internet voting systems. Outside of elections, policy, and technology, Benaloh recently completed 2 years as chair of the Sound Transit Citizen Oversight Panel, which oversees the Seattle regional transit authority that is currently investing billions annually on new infrastructure in the Puget Sound region.

KAREN COOK is the Ray Lyman Wilbur Professor of Sociology and vice provost for Faculty Development and Diversity at Stanford University. She is also the director of the Institute for Research in the Social Sciences (IRiSS) at Stanford and a trustee of the Russell Sage Foundation. Cook has a long-standing interest in social exchange, social networks, social justice, and trust in social relations. She has edited a number of books in the Russell Sage Foundation Trust Series including *Trust in Society* (2001), *Trust and Distrust in Organizations: Emerging Perspectives* (with R. Kramer, 2004), *eTrust: Forming Relations in the Online World* (with C. Snijders, V. Buskens, and Coye Cheshire, 2009), and *Whom Can Your Trust?* (with M. Levi and R. Hardin, 2009). She is co-author of *Cooperation without*

Trust? (with R. Hardin and M. Levi, 2005). In 1996, she was elected to the American Academy of Arts and Sciences and in 2007 to the National Academy of Sciences. In 2004 she received the ASA Social Psychology Section Cooley Mead Award for Career Contributions to Social Psychology.

DANA DeBEAUVOIR is in her 31st year serving as the elected Travis County Clerk in Austin, Texas. The Clerk's Office has a wide range of responsibilities including conducting elections; filing and preserving real property records; issuing marriage licenses; and managing civil, misdemeanor, and probate court records. With the passage of the Help America Vote Act in 2002, DeBeauvoir assumed new duties for the more than 130 local jurisdictions conducting their elections jointly with Travis County. She currently serves as the Texas representative on the federal Election Assistance Commission Standards Board, having served in that role since the position was established.

DeBeauvoir served as a United Nations Elections Observer at the 1994 election in South Africa that marked the end of apartheid. She served with the International Foundation for Electoral Systems as a consultant preparing for elections in Bangladesh (1995), Sarajevo, Bosnia (1996), and Pristina, Kosovo (1999). She also served as the Legislative Committee Chair for Elections for the County and District Clerks Association from 1995 to 2015. Her first award for improved management, a National Director's Award, presented by the International Association of Clerks, Recorders, Elections Officials, and Treasurers for creating a database of civil case names to cure an inherited and troublesome court backlog, was received in 1989. DeBeauvoir was awarded the 2009 Public Official of the Year by the National Association of County Recorders, Election Officials, and Clerks. The same year, she received the 2009 Minute Man Award for developing improved security practices by The Election Center. In 2014, she received the prestigious Eagle Award from The Election Center.

DeBeauvoir is a graduate of the University of Texas at Arlington, having received a B.A. in sociology/social work in 1979. She received a masters of public affairs in 1981 from the LBJ School of Public Affairs at the University of Texas at Austin. In 2002, she received the LBJ School Alumni Association Distinguished Public Service Award.

MOON DUCHIN is an associate professor in the Department of Mathematics and serves as founding director of the interdisciplinary Program in Science, Technology, and Society at Tufts University. Her mathematical research is in low-dimensional topology, geometric group theory, and dynamics. She leads a research team called the Metric Geometry and Gerrymandering Group (MGGG) that studies novel applications of geometry and topology to redistricting problems. One of the first public activities of the MGGG was a summer school in August 2017 that brought together scholars from law, civil rights, and mathematics to train expert witnesses for voting rights cases. Duchin is a fellow of the American Mathematical Society and holds a CAREER award from the National Science Foundation to study geometry at the intermediate scale between metric spaces and their asymptotic limits. She has lectured widely in pure mathematics and has spoken on the geometry of redistricting to audiences from high schools to a rabbinical school to the Distinguished Lecture Series of the Mathematical Association of America. She holds a Ph.D. in mathematics from the University of Chicago and a B.A. in mathematics and women's studies from Harvard University.

JUAN E. GILBERT is the Andrew Banks Family Preeminence Endowed Professor and chair of the Computer & Information Science & Engineering Department at the University of Florida where he leads the Human Experience Research Lab. He is also a fellow of the American Association of the Advancement of Science, a fellow of the National Academy of Inventors, an Association for Computing Machinery Distinguished Scientist, and a senior member of the Institue of Electrical and Electronics Engineers. Gilbert is the inventor of Prime III, an open-source, secure, and accessible voting technology that has been used in numerous organization elections and recently in statewide elections in New Hampshire.

SUSAN L. GRAHAM is the Pehong Chen Distinguished Professor of Electrical Engineering and Computer Science Emerita at the University of California, Berkeley. She received an A.B. in mathematics from Harvard University and M.S. and Ph.D. degrees in computer science from Stanford University. Her research has spanned programming language design and implementation, software tools, software development environments, and high-performance computing. She was the founding editor-in-chief of the Association for Computing Machinery (ACM) *Transactions on Programming Languages and Systems*. She is a fellow of the ACM, the Institute of Electrical and Electronics Engineers, and the American Academy of Arts and Sciences, and a member of the National Academy of Engineering.

Graham has served on numerous advisory and visiting committees and has been a consultant to a variety of companies. She was a member of the President's Information Technology Advisory Committee from 1997 to 2003. She served as the chief computer scientist for the National Partnership for Advanced Computational Infrastructure from 1997 to 2005. She was a member of the Harvard Board of Overseers from 2001 to 2007 and was president in 2006-2007. Graham was a founding member of the Computing Research Association's Computing Community Consortium, serving first as vice-chair and then as chair. From 2013 to January 2017 she was a member of the President's Council of Advisors on Science and Technology where she co-chaired their study and report "Big Data and Privacy: A Technological Perspective." She is a member of the Harvard Corporation (formally, a fellow of Harvard College).

NEAL KELLEY is registrar of voters for Orange County, California, the fifth largest voting jurisdiction in the United States, serving more than 1.6 million registered voters.

Kelley joined the county as chief deputy registrar of voters in 2004. In his role as the county's chief election official, he leads an organization responsible for conducting elections, verifying petitions, and maintaining voter records.

Prior to joining Orange County, Kelley developed and grew several companies of his own, employing hundreds of people from 1989 to 2004. He was also an adjunct professor with Riverside Community College's Business Administration Department, and served as a police officer in Southern California during the mid-1980s.

In 2009, Kelley earned professional election certification through the national Election Center and Auburn University as a Certified Elections and Registration Administrator. He has been the recipient of several awards for election administration, including recognition from the California State Association of Counties, The Election Center, and the National Association of Counties. He was recently honored with the "2015 Public Official of the Year" from the National Association of County Recorders, Election Officials and Clerks.

Kelley is an appointed member of the U.S. Election Assistance Commission Board of Advisors (and currently serves as chairman) and its Voting Systems Standards Board, is the past president of the California Association of Clerks and Election Officials, and is the immediate past president for the National Association of County Recorders, Election Officials, and Clerks.

Kelley earned a B.S. in business and management from the University of Redlands and an M.B.A. from the University of Southern California.

KEVIN J. KENNEDY left government service on June 29, 2016, with the dissolution of the Wisconsin Government Accountability Board. He presently consults and speaks on issues and topics related to campaign finance, elections, and ethics.

Kennedy served as director and General Counsel for the Wisconsin Government Accountability Board (G.A.B.) from November 5, 2007, through June 29, 2016. Before assuming the top staff position for the G.A.B., he was executive director—and before that legal counsel—for the Wisconsin State Elections Board.

Kennedy served as Wisconsin's chief election official from August 17,

1983 until June 29, 2016. No other individual has served longer in that capacity. Under his leadership, Wisconsin has been consistently recognized as a leader and innovator in the administration of elections, lobbying, and campaign finance.

In addition to his service to the people of Wisconsin, Kennedy has been active in a number of professional organizations. He has testified before Congress, several federal and state legislative bodies, and numerous private organizations active in the fields of campaign finance, elections, ethics, and lobbying.

NATHANIEL PERSILY is the James B. McClatchy Professor of Law at Stanford Law School, with appointments in the departments of Political Science and Communication. Prior to joining Stanford, Persily taught at Columbia and the University of Pennsylvania Law School, and as a visiting professor at Harvard, New York University, Princeton, the University of Amsterdam, and the University of Melbourne. Persily's scholarship and legal practice focus on American election law or what is sometimes called the "law of democracy," which addresses issues such as voting rights, political parties, campaign finance, redistricting, and election administration. He has served as a special master or court-appointed expert to craft congressional or legislative districting plans for Georgia, Maryland, Connecticut, and New York, and as the senior research director for the Presidential Commission on Election Administration. In addition to dozens of articles (many of which have been cited by the Supreme Court) on the legal regulation of political parties, issues surrounding the census and redistricting process, voting rights, and campaign finance reform. Persily is also coauthor of the leading election law casebook, *The Law of Democracy* (Foundation Press, 5th ed., 2016), with Samuel Issacharoff, Pamela Karlan, and Richard Pildes. His current work, for which he has been honored as an Andrew Carnegie Fellow, examines the impact of changing technology on political communication, campaigns, and election administration. He has edited several books, including *Public Opinion and Constitutional Controversy* (Oxford Press, 2008); *The Health Care Case: The Supreme Court's Decision and Its Implications* (Oxford Press 2013); and *Solutions to Political Polarization in America* (Cambridge Press, 2015). He received a B.A. and M.A. in political science from Yale (1992); a J.D. from Stanford (1998) where he was president of the *Stanford Law Review*; and a Ph.D. in political science from University of California, Berkeley in 2002.

RONALD L. RIVEST is an institute professor in the Massachusetts Institute of Technology's (MIT) Department of Electrical Engineering and Computer Science, and a leader of the Cryptography and Information Security research group within MIT's Computer Science and Artificial

Intelligence Laboratory. He received a B.A. in mathematics from Yale University in 1969 and a Ph.D. in computer science from Stanford University in 1974.

Rivest is a fellow of the Association for Computing Machinery and of the American Academy of Arts and Sciences and a member of the National Academy of Engineering and the National Academy of Sciences.

Rivest is an inventor of the RSA public-key cryptosystem and a founder of RSA Data Security. He has extensive experience in cryptographic design and cryptanalysis, and he has published numerous papers in these areas. He has served as director of the International Association for Cryptologic Research, the organizing body for the Eurocrypt and Crypto conferences, and of the Financial Cryptography Association. He has also worked extensively in the areas of computer algorithms and machine learning.

Rivest is a member of the CalTech/MIT Voting Technology Project and serves on the Board of Verified Voting. He has served on the TGDC (Technical Guidelines Development Committee) that advises the U.S. Election Assistance Commission and chaired the committee's subgroup on Security and Transparency.

CHARLES STEWART III is the Kenan Sahin Distinguished Professor of Political Science at the Massachusetts Institute of Technology (MIT), where he has taught since 1985, and a fellow of the American Academy of Arts and Sciences. His research and teaching areas include elections, congressional politics, and American political development.

Since 2001, Stewart has been a member of the Caltech/MIT Voting Technology Project, a leading research effort that applies scientific analysis to questions about election technology, election administration, and election reform. He is currently the MIT director of the project. In addition, he is the director of the MIT Election Data and Science Lab, a new initiative to disseminate scientific analysis of election processes among academic researchers and election practitioners. Stewart is an established leader in the analysis of the performance of election systems and the quantitative assessment of election performance. Working with the Pew Charitable Trusts, he helped with the development of Pew's Elections Performance Index. Stewart also provided advice to the Presidential Commission on Election Administration. His research on measuring the performance of elections and polling place operations is funded by Pew, the Democracy Fund, and the Hewlett Foundation. He recently published *The Measure of American Elections* (2014 with Barry C. Burden).

His current research about Congress touches on the historical development of committees, origins of partisan polarization, and Senate elections. His recent books of congressional research include *Electing the Senate*

(2014 with Wendy J. Schiller), *Fighting for the Speakership* (2012 with Jeffery A. Jenkins), and *Analyzing Congress* (2nd ed., 2011).

Stewart has been recognized at MIT for his undergraduate teaching, being named to the second class of MacVicar Fellows in 1994, awarded the Baker Award for Excellence in Undergraduate Teaching, and the recipient of the Class of 1960 Fellowship. From 1992 to 2015, he served as Head of House of McCormick Hall, along with his spouse, Kathryn M. Hess.

Stewart received his B.A. in political science from Emory University and S.M. and Ph.D. from Stanford University.

STAFF

ANNE-MARIE MAZZA, Ph.D., is the senior director of the Committee on Science, Technology, and Law. Mazza joined the National Academies of Sciences, Engineering, and Medicine in 1995. In 1999 she was named the first director of the Committee on Science, Technology, and Law. Mazza has been the study director on numerous National Academies' activities involving emerging technologies (e.g., human genome editing and synthetic biology), science in the courtroom (e.g., eyewitness identification and forensic science), and laws and regulations related to the governance of academic research (e.g., with regard to dual use research of concern, intellectual property, and human subjects). Between October 1999 and October 2000, Mazza divided her time between the National Academies and the White House Office of Science and Technology Policy, where she served as a senior policy analyst responsible for issues associated with a Presidential Review Directive on the government-university research partnership. Before joining the National Academies, Mazza was a senior consultant with Resource Planning Corporation. She is a fellow of the American Association for the Advancement of Science. Mazza was awarded a B.A., M.A., and Ph.D. from The George Washington University.

JON EISENBERG is the senior board director of the Computer Science and Telecommunications Board of the National Academies of Sciences, Engineering, and Medicine. He has been study director for a diverse body of work, including a series of studies exploring Internet and broadband policy and networking and communications technologies. In 1995-1997 he was an American Association for the Advancement of Science, Engineering, and Diplomacy Fellow at the U.S. Agency for International Development, where he worked on technology transfer and information and telecommunications policy issues. Eisenberg received his Ph.D. in physics from the University of Washington in 1996 and B.S. in physics with honors from the University of Massachusetts at Amherst in 1988.

STEVEN KENDALL is program officer for the Committee on Science, Technology, and Law. Dr. Kendall has contributed to numerous National Academies of Sciences, Engineering, and Medicine reports, including *Dual Use Research of Concern in the Life Sciences: Current Issues and Controversies* (2017); *Optimizing the Nation's Investment in Academic Research* (2016); *International Summit on Human Gene Editing: A Global Discussion* (2015); *Identifying the Culprit: Assessing Eyewitness Identification* (2014); *Positioning Synthetic Biology to Meet the Challenges of the 21st Century* (2013); the *Reference Manual on Scientific Evidence*, 3rd Edition (2011); *Review of the Scientific Approaches Used During the FBI's Investigation of the 2001 Anthrax Mailings* (2011); *Managing University Intellectual Property in the Public Interest* (2010); and *Strengthening Forensic Science in the United States: A Path Forward* (2009). Kendall completed his Ph.D. in the Department of the History of Art and Architecture at the University of California, Santa Barbara, where he wrote a dissertation on 19th century British painting. Kendall received his M.A. in Victorian art and architecture at the University of London. Prior to joining the National Research Council in 2007, he worked at the Smithsonian American Art Museum and The Huntington in San Marino, California.

KAROLINA KONARZEWSKA is program coordinator for the Committee on Science, Technology, and Law. She holds a master's degree in applied economics from George Mason University, a master's degree in international relations from New York University, and a bachelor's degree in political science from the College of Staten Island, City University of New York. Prior to joining the National Academies of Sciences, Engineering, and Medicine, she worked at various research institutions in Washington, DC, where she covered political and economic issues pertaining to Europe, Russia, and Eurasia.

WILLIAM J. SKANE is former executive director of the Office of News and Public Information at the National Academies of Sciences, Engineering, and Medicine. He retired in 2017, having assumed the position in 2002. Before joining the Academies, Skane was the Washington producer for the CBS News broadcast *Sunday Morning with Charles Kuralt* (1991-2002) and national medical producer for the *CBS Evening News with Dan Rather* (1984-1991). He is the recipient of three Emmy awards, two Peabody awards, a Sigma Delta Chi award for breaking news coverage, and the Westinghouse-AAAS award for science reporting on television. Skane began his journalism career as the science reporter for public television station KQED in San Francisco. He earned an Honors B.A. in economics from Stanford University, an M.J. from the Graduate School of Journalism at the University of California, Berkeley, and an M.Ed. from The George Washington University.

Appendix B

Committee Meeting Agendas

Meeting 1
Washington, DC
April 4-5, 2017

TUESDAY, APRIL 4, 2017

OPEN SESSION

10:00 AM   Welcome/Introductions/Meeting Overview

Committee Co-Chairs:

Lee C. Bollinger, Columbia University
Michael A. McRobbie, Indiana University

10:15 AM   Hand-off of Study from Co-Chairs of Committee on Science, Technology, and Law

Speakers:

David Baltimore, California Institute of Technology
David S. Tatel, U.S. Court of Appeals for the District of Columbia Circuit

10:30 AM   Charge to the Committee

           Speaker:

           Geri Mannion, Carnegie Corporation of New York

10:45 AM   Overview of the U.S. Election Process

           Speaker:

           Thad Hall, Fors Marsh Group

11:15 AM   Q&A with Committee

12 noon   Lunch

1:00 PM   Overview of Voting Technologies

           Speakers:

           Brian Newby and Jessica Myers, U.S. Election Assistance
           Commission

1:20 PM   Q&A with Committee

2:00 PM   Voting Equipment as a Critical National Infrastructure

           Speaker:

           Geoffrey Hale, U.S. Department of Homeland Security

2:20 PM   Q&A with Committee

3:00 PM   Break

3:15 PM   Issues Arising from the 2016 Presidential Election

           Speaker:

           Alex Padilla, National Association of Secretaries of State

3:35 PM   Q&A with Committee

4:10 PM   The View of Elections at the Local Level

           Speaker:

           David Stafford, Escambia County, FL

4:30 PM   Q&A with Committee

5:00 PM   Adjourn to Closed Session

WEDNESDAY, APRIL 5, 2017

OPEN SESSION

10:00 AM   2014 Report and Recommendations of the Presidential
           Commission on Election Administration

           Speaker:

           Robert F. Bauer, Perkins Coie LLP

10:20 AM   Q&A with Committee

11:00 AM   Challenges Ahead: View from the U.S. Election Assistance
           Commission

           Speaker:

           Matthew Masterson, U.S. Election Assistance Commission

11:20 AM   Q&A with Committee

12 noon   Adjourn to Closed Session

Meeting 2
New York, NY
June 12-13, 2017

MONDAY, JUNE 12, 2017

OPEN SESSION

10:00 AM   Welcome/Introductions/Meeting Overview

Committee Co-Chairs:

Lee C. Bollinger, Columbia University
Michael A. McRobbie, Indiana University

10:10 AM   Increasing Vulnerability: Security Challenges

Speakers:

J. Alex Halderman, University of Michigan
Alexander Schwarzmann, University of Connecticut

10:45 AM   Q&A with Committee

11:15 AM   The Market for Election Equipment and Technology: What's
Stopping Innovation?

Speaker:

Matthew Caulfied, University of Pennsylvania

11:35 AM   Q&A with Committee

12:00 PM   Lunch

12:45 PM   Technology Challenges Facing Election Administrators

Speakers:

Douglas A. Kellner, State of New York
Peggy Reeves, State of Connecticut
Robert Rock, State of Rhode Island

> Will Senning, State of Vermont
> Anthony Stevens, State of New Hampshire

2:15 PM   Q&A with Committee

3:15 PM   Break

3:30 PM   Rapidly Evolving Voting Technology

Speakers:

> Merle King, Center for Elections Systems, Kennesaw
> State University
> Lawrence Norden, Brennan Center for Justice at New
> York University

4:00 PM   Q&A with Committee

4:30 PM   Adjourn to Closed Session

TUESDAY, JUNE 13, 2017

OPEN SESSION

8:00 AM   Continental Breakfast

8:30 AM   Welcome and Introductions

Committee Co-Chairs:

> Lee C. Bollinger, Columbia University
> Michael A. McRobbie, Indiana University

8:45 AM   Accessibility: Challenges to Access for All

Speakers:

> Lisa Schur, Rutgers University
> Diane Cordry Golden, Association of Assistive
> Technology Act Programs
> Whitney Quesenbery, Center for Civic Design

9:30 AM   Q&A with Committee

10:15 AM   Adjourn to Closed Session

Meeting 3
Washington, DC
October 18-19, 2017

WEDNESDAY, OCTOBER 18, 2017

OPEN SESSION

8:30 AM   Continental Breakfast

9:00 AM   Welcome/Introductions/Meeting Overview

           Committee Co-Chairs:

               Lee C. Bollinger, Columbia University
               Michael A. McRobbie, Indiana University

9:05 AM   National Security and National Elections

           Speaker:

               General Michael Hayden, U.S. Air Force, National
                   Security Agency, and Central Intelligence Agency
                   (retired)

9:30 AM   Q&A with Committee

10:10 AM   Update from U.S. Department of Homeland Security on
           Cyber Attacks During the 2016 Election and Critical
           Infrastructure Policy

           Speaker:

               Robert Kolasky, U.S. Department of Homeland Security

10:35 AM   Q&A with Committee

11:00 AM   Cybersecurity Attacks: Understanding Attacks, Threats, and
Policy Options

Speakers:

Matthew Blaze, University of Pennsylvania
Susan Hennessey, Brookings Institution
David Fidler, Indiana University

11:45 AM   Q&A with Committee

12:15 PM   Adjourn to Closed Session

OPEN SESSION

2:30 PM   Election Vendors: Current Trends and a View of the Future

Speakers:

Jonathan Brill, Scytl
Jackie Harris, Democracy Live
John Schmitt, Five Cedars Group
James Simons, Everyone Counts

3:30 PM   Q&A with Committee

4:00 PM   Break

4:15 PM   Demonstration by Election Systems Vendors

5:15 PM   Adjourn to Closed Session

THURSDAY, OCTOBER 19, 2017

OPEN SESSION

8:00 AM   Continental Breakfast

8:30 AM   Welcome and Introductions

           Committee Co-Chairs:

               Lee C. Bollinger, Columbia University
               Michael A. McRobbie, Indiana University

8:40 AM   Overseas and Military Voting

           Speaker:

               David Beirne, Federal Voting Assistance Program

9:00 AM   Q&A with Committee

9:30 AM   Maintaining and Updating Voter Registration Databases

           Speakers:

               David Becker, Center for Election Innovation & Research
               Shane Hamlin, Electronic Registration Information
                  Center (ERIC)
               Edgardo Cortes, State of Virginia Elections Board

10:00 AM   Q&A with Committee

10:30 AM   Voluntary Voting System Standard 2.0

           Speaker:

               Mary Brady, National Institute of Standards and
                  Technology

10:50 AM   Q&A with Committee

11:15 AM   Adjourn to Closed Session

Meeting 4
Denver, CO
December 7-8, 2017

THURSDAY, DECEMBER 7, 2017

OPEN SESSION

11:00 AM   Welcome/Introductions/Meeting Overview

Committee Co-Chairs:

Lee C. Bollinger, Columbia University
Michael A. McRobbie, Indiana University

11:10 AM   Mail-in Ballots: The Oregon Experience

Speaker:

Brenda Bayes, State of Oregon

11:30 AM   Q&A with Committee

12 noon   Lunch

1:00 PM   Voting: The Colorado Experience

Speakers:

Jennifer Morrell, Arapahoe County, CO
Hillary Hall, Boulder County, CO
Amber McReynolds, City and County of Denver, CO –
via videoconference

1:45 PM   Q&A with Committee

2:15 PM   Voting: The Los Angeles County Experience

Speakers:

Kenneth Bennett, Los Angeles County, CA – via
videoconference
Monica Flores, Los Angeles County, CA – via videoconference

2:30 PM   Q&A with Committee

2:45 PM   Break

3:00 PM   Vote Centers

            Speakers:

                Robert M. Stein, Rice University
                Joe P. Gloria, Clark County, NV

3:30 PM   Q&A with Committee

4:00 PM   Adjourn to Closed Session

FRIDAY, DECEMBER 8, 2017

OPEN SESSION

7:30 AM   Continental Breakfast

8:00 AM   Welcome and Introductions

            Committee Co-Chairs:

                Lee C. Bollinger, Columbia University
                Michael A. McRobbie, Indiana University

8:15 AM   Election Vendors: Current Trends and a View of the Future

            Speakers:

                Eddie Perez, Hart InterCivic
                McDermot Coutts, Unisyn Voting Solutions

9:00 AM   Q&A with Committee

9:30 AM   Risk-limiting Audits

Speakers:

Joe Kiniry, Free & Fair – via videoconference
Neal McBurnett, Independent Election Integrity Consultant;
   Free & Fair
Hilary Rudy, State of Colorado

10:15 AM   Q&A with Committee

10:45 AM   Break

11:00 AM   Education/Training/Professionalization of the Election Workforce

Speakers:

Tim Mattice, The Election Center
Kathleen Hale, Auburn University
Doug Chapin, University of Minnesota – via videoconference

11:30 AM   Q&A with Committee

12:00 PM   Adjourn to Closed Session

Meeting 5
Washington, DC
February 21-22, 2018

WEDNESDAY, FEBRUARY 21, 2018

OPEN SESSION

8:30 AM   Continental Breakfast

9:00 AM   Welcome and Introductions

Committee Co-Chairs:

Lee C. Bollinger, Columbia University
Michael A. McRobbie, Indiana University

9:05 AM   Lessons Learned from the 2016 Election: An Update

Speakers:

Connie Lawson, Secretary of State of the State of Indiana
and President, National Association of Secretaries of
State – via videoconference
Leslie Reynolds, Executive Director, National Association
of Secretaries of State

9:30 AM   Q&A with Committee

10:00 AM   Adjourn to Closed Session

THURSDAY, FEBRUARY 22, 2018

CLOSED SESSION

Meeting 6
New York, NY
June 20, 2018

MEETING CLOSED IN ITS ENTIRETY

Appendix C

The Targeting of the American Electorate

In an assessment of Russian activities related to the 2016 presidential election, members of the the U.S. intelligence community[1] found that:

> We assess Russian President Vladimir Putin ordered an influence campaign in 2016 aimed at the US presidential election. Russia's goals were to undermine public faith in the US democratic process, denigrate Secretary Clinton, and harm her electability and potential presidency. We further assess Putin and the Russian Government developed a clear preference for President-elect Trump. We have high confidence in these judgments.[2]

The report concluded:

> Russian efforts to influence the 2016 US presidential election represent the most recent expression of Moscow's longstanding desire to undermine the US-led liberal democratic order, but these activities demonstrated a significant escalation in directness, level of activity, and scope of effort compared to previous operations.[3]

---

[1] In this case, the Federal Bureau of Investigation, the Central Intelligence Agency, and the National Security Agency.

[2] Office of the Director of National Intelligence, "Assessing Russian Activities and Intentions in Recent US Elections, Intelligence Community Assessment," January 6, 2017, p. ii, available at: https://www.dni.gov/files/documents/ICA_2017_01.pdf. Boldface text is original to the document.

[3] Ibid.
The report also stated that the agencies "assess Putin and the Russian Government aspired to help President-elect Trump's election chances when possible by discrediting Secretary Clinton

Social media companies later reported that, during the 2016 presidential campaign, Russian state operatives had purchased large numbers of online political ads targeting narrow segments of the American population. Facebook provided Congressional investigators with information regarding 3,000 paid ads linked to Russia.[4] Twitter identified hundreds of Russian accounts and revealed that the Russian RT news site had purchased $274,100 in online ads in 2016.[5] Google also identified Russian-bought ads aimed at influencing the 2016 election on YouTube, Gmail, and other platforms.[6]

In October 2017, Nikki Haley, U.S. Ambassador to the United Nations," stated that when a "country can . . . interfere in another country's elections, that is warfare." Misinformation creates a situation where "democracy shifts [away] from what the people want. We didn't just see it here. You can look at France, and you can look at other countries. They [Russia] are doing this everywhere. This is their new weapon of choice. And we have to make sure we get in front of it. . . . Our Intelligence agencies

---

and publicly contrasting her unfavorably to him. All three agencies agree with this judgment. CIA and FBI have high confidence in this judgment; NSA has moderate confidence;" that "Moscow's approach evolved over the course of the campaign based on Russia's understanding of the electoral prospects of the two main candidates. When it appeared to Moscow that Secretary Clinton was likely to win the election, the Russian influence campaign began to focus more on undermining her future presidency;" that "further information has come to light since Election Day that, when combined with Russian behavior since early November 2016, increases our confidence in our assessments of Russian motivations and goals;" that "Moscow's influence campaign followed a Russian messaging strategy that blends covert intelligence operations—such as cyber activity—with overt efforts by Russian Government agencies, state-funded media, third-party intermediaries, and paid social media users or 'trolls.' Russia, like its Soviet predecessor, has a history of conducting covert influence campaigns focused on US presidential elections that have used intelligence officers and agents and press placements to disparage candidates perceived as hostile to the Kremlin;" that "Russia's intelligence services conducted cyber operations against targets associated with the 2016 US presidential election, including targets associated with both major US political parties;" and that "We assess with high confidence that Russian military intelligence (General Staff Main Intelligence Directorate or GRU) used the Guccifer 2.0 persona and DCLeaks.com to release US victim data obtained in cyber operations publicly and in exclusives to media outlets and relayed material to WikiLeaks . . . Russia's state-run propaganda machine contributed to the influence campaign by serving as a platform for Kremlin messaging to Russian and international audiences." (See pp. ii-iii).

[4] Shane, Scott, "Facebook to Turn Over Russian-linked ads to Congress," *New York Times*, September 21, 2017.

[5] Dwoskin, Elizabeth, Adam Entous, and Karoun Demirjian, "Twitter Finds Hundreds of Accounts Tied to Russian Operatives," *Washington Post*, September 28, 2017.

[6] Dwoskin, Elizabeth, Adam Entous, and Craig Timberg "Google Uncovers Russian-Bought Ads on Youtube, Gmail and Other Platforms," *Washington Post*, October 9, 2017.

are working overtime now because there's just so much when it comes to cyber threats . . . that we are having to deal with."[7,8]

As political scientist Francis Fukuyama noted in a report to the U.S. Department of State, "the speed and scale of today's 'weaponization of information' is unprecedented . . . falsehood often travels faster than truth, leaving context and provenance behind. The traditional answer to the spread of bad information has been to inject good information . . . on the assumption that the truth would rise to the top. . . . In a world of trolls and bots, where simple facts are instantly countered by automated agents, this strategy may not be adequate. It is unclear how effectively democratic societies can continue to deliberate and function, and how hostile foreign actors can be identified and neutralized."[9]

---

[7] Haley, Nikki, panel with Nikki Haley, U.S. Ambassador to the United Nations and former Secretaries of State Madeleine Albright and Condoleezza Rice. The panel was part of a forum titled "The Spirit of Liberty: At Home, In the World" focused on freedom, free markets, and security and hosted by the George W. Bush Institute in New York City on October 19, 2017. Video of the panel is available at: https://www.c-span.org/video/?435568-3/ambassador-haley-secretaries-albright-rice-discuss-us-role-world&start=1885.

[8] More recently, James Clapper, former Director of National Intelligence, remarked, "As a private citizen, it's what I would call my informed opinion that, given the massive effort the Russians made, and the number of citizens that they touched, and the variety and multidimensional aspects of what they did to influence opinion . . . and given the fact that it turned on less than 80,000 votes in three states, to me it exceeds logic and credulity that they didn't affect the election. And it's my belief they actually turned it." See Sargent, Greg, "James Clapper's Bombshell: Russia Swung the Election. What If He's Right?," *Washington Post,* May 24, 2018.

[9] U.S. Advisory Commission on Public Diplomacy, *Can Public Diplomacy Survive the Internet? Bots, Echochambers, and Disinformation,* edited by Shawn Powers and Markos Kounalakis, May 2017, available at: https://www.state.gov/documents/organization/271028.pdf.

Appendix D

The Cost of Election Administration in the United States

Determining the cost of the administration of national elections is difficult. In 2001, the Caltech/MIT Voting Technology Project (VTP), in a comprehensive report about election administration in the United States, stated:

> Even the most basic facts about the cost and finance of elections in the United States are unavailable, and the most basic questions remain unexamined. It is not known how much we spend on election administration overall in the U.S. each year. It is not known on what funds are spent. There has been little analysis of how and how well local governments provide election services. Each of us has some sense of what we get—a stable and successful democracy. But there are clearly problems that can be remedied. How much will improvements in this system cost? [1]

There is general agreement that this assessment remains applicable.

The VTP conducted a survey of local elections officials in an attempt to determine the cost of conducting the 2000 presidential election. Based upon the information received from respondents, the cost was estimated to be $1 billion. The survey was repeated by the VTP in 2013 on behalf of the Presidential Commission on Election Administration, and the result was of a similar order of magnitude: around $2.6 billion.[2]

---

[1] Caltech/MIT Voting Technology Project, "Voting – What Is, What Could Be," 2001, p. 48, available at: http://vote.caltech.edu/reports/1.

[2] See http://web.mit.edu/supportthevoter/www/2013/12/11/pcea-public-meeting-december-3-2013-webcast-materials/.

There is little scholarly literature on the subject. The literature typically comments on the lack of comparable data, not only across states, but also often within government units across time.[3] The U.S. Census Bureau's "Census of Government" does not inquire specifically about election administration. The National Conference of State Legislatures recently reported that only four states (California, Colorado, North Dakota, and Wisconsin) collect statewide cost data.[4]

As a general matter, localities are responsible for financially supporting elections, but how that works in practice varies across states. States typically contribute funds to support election administration. In general, states tend to be most financially and administratively responsible for voter registration systems and localities tend have financial and administrative responsibility for staff, personnel, rent, etc. In many states, the cost of voting technology is shared between the state and localities. Some states (e.g., Rhode Island) centralize the purchase of voting technology.[5]

The federal government has played a role in the funding of elections. Federal funding for elections has been episodic and typically focused on particular projects, such as support for the purchase of new voting equipment or for security enhancements. As discussed, federal funds have been disbursed by the U.S. Election Assistance Commission (EAC). There have been discussions of an annual appropriation to states to assist with the "federal portion" of the state and local election administration, but the proposal has not gained traction.

The federal government provides support for the EAC and the National Institute of Standards and Technology (NIST). That funding is currently less than $10 million/year.[6] The federal government also provides support for the Federal Voter Assistance Program (FVAP). That funding ranges from $3.5 million to $4.0 million per year. These allocations represent the only ongoing support provided by the federal government for election administration.

---

[3] That literature includes Montjoy, Robert S., "The Changing Nature . . . and Costs . . . of Election Administration," *Public Administration Review*, 2010, Vol. 70, No. 6, pp. 867-875 and Hill, Sarah, "Election Administration Finance in California Counties," *The American Review of Public Administration*, 2012, Vol. 42, No. 5, pp. 606-628.

[4] See http://www.ncsl.org/research/elections-and-campaigns/the-price-of-democracy-splitting-the-bill-for-elections.aspx.

[5] For recent discussions on the topic of funding elections, see the three reports released by the National Conference of State Legislatures ("The Price of Democracy: Splitting the Bill for Elections;" "Election Costs: What States Pay;" and "Funding Elections Technology") in 2018.

[6] See https://www.eac.gov/assets/1/6/FY_2019_CBJ_Feb_12_2018_FINAL.pdf.

Appendix E

Reasons to Cast a Provisional Ballot

Reason	States
Voter eligibility cannot be immediately established—i.e., name is not on registration list	45 States + DC: Alabama, Alaska, Arizona, Arkansas, California, Colorado, Connecticut, Delaware, District of Columbia, Florida, Georgia, Hawaii, Illinois, Indiana, Iowa, Kansas, Kentucky, Louisiana, Maine, Maryland, Massachusetts, Michigan, Mississippi, Missouri, Montana, Nebraska, Nevada, New Jersey, New Mexico, New York, North Carolina, Ohio, Oklahoma, Oregon, Pennsylvania, Rhode Island, South Carolina, South Dakota, Tennessee, Texas, Utah, Vermont, Virginia, Washington, West Virginia, Wyoming
The voter's eligibility is challenged by a poll watcher	26 States + DC: Alabama, Alaska, Arizona, Colorado, Connecticut, Delaware, District of Columbia, Florida, Illinois, Indiana, Iowa, Kansas, Kentucky, Louisiana, Maine, Maryland, Montana, Nevada, Ohio, Pennsylvania, Rhode Island, South Carolina, South Dakota, Tennessee, Utah, West Virginia, Wyoming
Voter did not present ID as required by the state	36 States + DC: Alabama, Alaska, Arizona, Arkansas, Colorado, Connecticut, District of Columbia, Florida, Georgia, Illinois, Indiana, Iowa, Kansas, Kentucky, Louisiana, Maine, Maryland, Massachusetts, Michigan, Mississippi, Montana, Nebraska, Nevada, New Jersey, New Mexico, New York, North Carolina, Ohio, Oklahoma, Pennsylvania, Rhode Island, Tennessee, Texas, Utah, Virginia, Washington, Wisconsin
Voter requested a by-mail ballot and has not cast it	16 States + DC: Alabama, Arizona, Arkansas, California, District of Columbia, Illinois, Kansas, Maryland, Montana, Nebraska, Nevada, New Jersey, Ohio, Rhode Island, Texas, Virginia, Washington

continued

155

Reason	States
Registration reflects an error in party listing (primary election only)	10 States + DC: California, District of Columbia, Maine, Maryland, Massachusetts, New Jersey, New York, North Carolina, Oklahoma, Pennsylvania, West Virginia
Address and/or name has changed	9 States + DC: Alaska, Arizona, California, District of Columbia, Florida, Maryland, Mississippi, New Jersey, Ohio, Texas

SOURCE: National Conference of State Legislatures, "Provisional Ballots," available at: http://www.ncsl.org/research/elections-and-campaigns/lb-provisional-ballots.aspx.

Appendix F

Acronyms and Abbreviations

ADA	Americans with Disabilities Act of 1990
ATM	Automatic teller machine
AVR	Automatic voter registration
BMD	Ballot-marking device
CAC	Common Access Card
CDF	Common Data Format
COTS	Commercial off-the-shelf
CVR	Cast vote record
DHS	U.S. Department of Homeland Security
DMV	Department of motor vehicles
DoD	U.S. Department of Defense
DoS	Denial-of-service
DRE	Direct Recording Electronic
E2E	End-to-end
E2E-V	End-to-end-verifiable
EAC	U.S. Election Assistance Commission
EAVS	Election Administration and Voting Survey
EI-ISAC	Election Infrastructure Information Sharing and Analysis Center
EPB	Electronic pollbook

ERIC	Electronic Registration Information Center
ES&S	Election Systems and Software
FEC	Federal Election Commission
FVAP	Federal Voting Assistance Program
GAO	U.S. Government Accountability Office
HAVA	Help America Vote Act of 2002
ISAC	Information Sharing and Analysis Center
IT	Information technology
MOVE	Military and Oversees Voter Empowerment Act of 2009
MPSA	Military Postal Service Agency
NAE	National Academy of Engineering
NAM	National Academy of Medicine
NAS	National Academy of Sciences
NASPAA	Network of Schools of Public Policy, Affairs, and Administration
NASS	National Association of Secretaries of State
NCLS	National Conference of State Legislatures
NIST	U.S. National Institute of Standards and Technology
NSF	U.S. National Science Foundation
NVRA	National Voter Registration Act of 1993
ODNI	Office of the Director of National Intelligence
RFP	Request for proposals
RLA	Risk-limiting audit
SSA	U.S. Social Security Administration
STAR Vote	Secure, Transparent, Auditable Reliable Vote
UOCAVA	Uniformed and Overseas Citizens Absentee Voting Act of 1986
USPS	U.S. Postal Service
VAEHA	Voting Accessibility for the Elderly and Handicapped Act of 1984
VR	Voter registration
VRA	Voting Rights Act of 1965
VRD	Voter registration database

VSAP	Voting Solutions for All People (formerly the Voting System Assessment Project)
VSTL	Voting system testing laboratories
VTP	Caltech/MIT Voting Technology Project
VVPAT	Voter-verifiable paper audit trail
VVSG	Voluntary Voting System Guidelines